Scandinavians

ARE VERY MODEST PEOPLE

BUT THEY HAVE MUCH TO BE MODEST ABOUT, THEN

by Art Lee

Author of **Real Scandinavians Never Ask Directions,
The Lutefisk Ghetto, Leftover Lutefisk** and **Leftover Lefse.**

A special thanks to Christine and Richard Hefte for both proof-reading and "tweaking" the final manuscript.

Photo credits:
Iola Historical Society 16, 19, 22, 23, 27
Art Lee 63, 65, 68, 71, 85, 119, 140
Ted Thorson 127

"Singing With the Lutherans" by Garrison Keillor (pg.132) reproduced with permission.

Published by
Adventure Publications, Inc.
820 Cleveland Street South
Cambridge, MN 55008
1-800-678-7006

ISBN: 1-59193-092-8

"Once I thought to write a history of the immigrants to America. And then I discovered that immigrants were American History."

Oscar Handlin
Harvard University

Plans Aforethought . . .

The Book's Title and an Explanation, of Sorts

SCANDINAVIANS ARE VERY MODEST PEOPLE
But They Have Much To Be Modest About, Then

The main title is a common statement made about Scandinavians and the author believes that comment is correct. Carried further, Scandinavian Americans, like their forbears, are also very modest people. The subtitle, however, the author believes is not true. More on both opinions in the later sections of the book.

As to the somewhat strange word order of the subtitle, the author is having a little fun with the Scandinavian inclination to end their sentences with the word "then." Common examples: "Are you going to town today, then?" Answer: "Well maybe, maybe not, then."

Some of this penchant for the "then" endings derives from the Scandinavian word for then, namely "da." It was and is still common for native speakers to answer a question in the affirmative by saying quickly "Ja da" (yes, then), not just a plain "Ja." That penchant got carried over into Scandinavian English, then. Readers may in the future want to do a quick reinterpretation when they again hear the phrase "Uff da."

The author hopes that this commentary is useful, then.

Informative and Interesting

In some 50 years of teaching school—from junior high kids to college graduate students to Elderhostel folks—it seems to me that almost all students of any age wanted the same things: to learn something and have it be interesting while learning, if not fun.

There are no dull subjects, just dull teachers. (I heard a rumor once that math could be interesting, but I never personally experienced it.) This concept of "interesting information" was my approach as a classroom teacher as well as a writer. Success in this area, of course, is determined by the students and the readers.

This book, *Scandinavians . . .* tries to achieve that concept, as clearly some items are just for entertainment (indeed, pretty silly at times) and some sections are essentially didactic (look it up); and some sections try to combine the two.

Scandinavians, my fifth book, tells about growing up in a country town before, during and after the most significant event of the 20th century: World War II. Whether this was a typical and representative American community at the time is for the reader to decide.

Outsiders, then, looking at us in our town, and readers today drawing their own conclusions after perusing this prose might both agree that altogether we lived lives that were extraordinarily uneventful. True. We suspected as much at the time, but hey, that was all we had, all we knew; it was home!

In this overall growing experience came an overall message seeping through that has served me well over a lifetime: You simply live your life as well as you can in all its strangely compelling mundaneness. Persevere.

–Art Lee

TABLE OF CONTENTS

Everything You Wanted To Know About . . . Lutherans

1. Lutherans like to sing except when confronted with a new hymn or a hymn with more than four stanzas.

2. Lutherans believe in prayer, but would practically die if asked to pray out loud, other than "Come, Lord Jesus, Be Our Guest."

3. Lutherans usually follow the official "green book" liturgy and feel slighted and slightly lost when substitutions are made.

4. Lutherans believe that pastors will visit them in the hospital even if no one notifies the pastors that they are there. Pastors are just supposed to know.

5. Lutherans feel that applauding for the children's choirs in church is all right, but not so for the senior choir.

6. Lutherans believe that regardless of the quality of the sermon, no one can be saved after 20 minutes.

7. Lutherans assume that the Bible forbids folks from crossing the middle aisle while "passing the peace."

8. Lutherans believe it is proper to sit in the same pew every Sunday, because when they look around at any empty pew, they know who's missing.

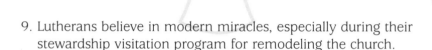

9. Lutherans believe in modern miracles, especially during their stewardship visitation program for remodeling the church.

10. Lutherans believe that new pastors who show up sporting beards, goatees and/or moustaches are automatically suspect from the start.

11. Lutherans believe that if you show up for an event at the exact starting time, you're late.

12. Lutherans never let their faces show what their minds are thinking.

13. Lutherans on Social Security believe that the only paid position in the operation of a church should be that of the pastor; all other jobs should be done by volunteers.

14. Lutherans believe if you don't say anything, then you don't have to explain yourself.

"Wherever there are two or more
gathered together . . .
    an offering will be taken."

Growing Up Unconfused

THE CONFUSION CAME LATER

One's ethnic heritage is hardly appreciated, let alone understood, when one is a child. The life-style you lead and see all around you every day just seems ordinary and natural at the time. (Doesn't everyone have lutefisk for Christmas Eve supper?)

You silently, unquestionably absorb the culture over the years, seldom aware of anything special or decidedly different about your surroundings and the people who surround you. Yet that special way-of-life, of thinking, acting, doing/not doing seems to have seeped into every pore of your being. It's like osmosis; you almost inhale it from the Scandinavian-filled air you breathe. In this ethereal (read: indoctrination) process, no person has ever set you down and explained, "Well, this is the way it is, then, and the way it's supposed to be; this is how you are to live your life now and forevermore. Amen."

As a result, you just grow and accept it all, probably like Topsy in *Uncle Tom's Cabin*, but in this case more like Torvold in *Uncle Lars' Farmhouse*.

A sampling of things that rural Scandinavian kids absorbed in those formative years both before and after World War II:

- If you really want anything to get done, do it yourself.
- Never brag. Never. Never. Never.
- If you go outside with a wet head, you'll catch your death of a cold.

- A girl's education in The Dirty Thirties was not complete without proper training in housekeeping, cooking, baking and infant care, all in preparation for their becoming domestic servants for some rich city family. (P.S. Girls should stay around home and become a secretary or a clerk or a telephone operator.)

- A boy's education in the Depression years stops after eighth grade. Well, maybe high school at the most; seeing one can't find a job anyway, might as well mark time at this higher ed stuff. (P.S. If you're big enough to work, work.)

- Never complain about the cards you're dealt. Life—and cards—may be unfair, but don't complain about it. (Trust everybody, but cut the cards.)

- A traffic jam is defined as a situation where four cars have trouble passing a tractor on a county road.

- During the fall butchering season, the critter's blood is to be caught in buckets and brought to the kitchen where it is turned into a form of blood pudding called "klub." The blood is mixed with chopped onions, eggs, breadcrumbs, salt, pepper, suet, sugar and flour. The mixture is placed in baking pans and cooked for one hour and then served as the entrée for suppers. So what's so different about that?

- Avoid confrontations. Despite provocations, be solid, stolid and silent. The agreed upon illusion in life is stability.

- Learn your euphemisms; they work well. For example, when someone or some thing is declared "different," it means that person or thing is goofier than an outhouse rat.

- Being Lutheran is Normal, probably even Natural and certainly Biblically correct. As for those people in those other strange cults, well . . . they're "different."

- Hollywood is nothing more than a high class whorehouse.

- Take on your plate only what food you can eat. Clean up everything on your plate. If you don't, then think about all those starving children in Madagascar.

- Internalize your emotions. If sad, tough it out on your own. If happy, don't let it show too much. Either way, say nothing.

- To be average is good. To be too good is bad. Strive to be average.

- When in doubt, don't.

- Make no phone calls after 10:00 p.m., the hour the world stops. And a long distance call any time of the day or night is a sure sign that something awful has happened.

- The town pastor is the most important, intelligent, prestigious person in the community. Just don't socialize with him.

- There are few joys in life that equal the very last day of school.

REST IN PEACE, PLEASE . . .
AND HURRY UP ABOUT IT

A woman accompanied her husband to the doctor's office. After his checkup, the doctor called the wife into his office alone. He said, "Your husband is a very sick man, suffering from a severe disease, combined with horrible stress. If you do not do the following, your husband will surely die."

The doctor then told her: "Each morning, get up before he does and fix him a hearty breakfast. Always be pleasant, and work to get him in a good mood. Never contradict him. For lunch fix him a healthy meal. Insist he take a nap each day. For dinner prepare an especially nice meal for him each day. Don't burden him with any chores. Never discuss your own problems with him; it will only make his stress worse. Never find fault with anything he says or does. And most importantly, make love with your husband several times a week and satisfy his every fantasy.

"If you do this for the next ten months to a year, I think your husband will live several more years."

On the way home, the husband asked his wife, "What did the doctor tell you?"

She replied, "You're going to die soon."

Setting The Stage

At this point a short introduction to my hometown may be useful, both to inform and maybe spark a tiny interest in rural Midwest towns and their pattern of growth and decline. Because this book was preceded by four others—*The Lutefisk Ghetto*, *Leftover Lutefisk*, *Leftover Lefse*, and *Real Scandinavians Never Ask Directions*—all of which deal largely with the life and times of this one community, a brief intro to the town of Scandinavia seems necessary. Let us begin with a prologue, a tantalizing attempt to engage the reader in small town America.

Prologue

Even now in the 21st century we carry images of the small-town American countryside deep in the mind. That mind-view conjures up scenes of red barns, lush farm crops in rolling fields, cows grazing in green pastures, and all this bucolic activity amid picturesque little lakes and rippling streams, backgrounded by big pines and fat, gnarly oak trees. An impressive picture, this restful, rural dream-image shows up in a variety of ways and is often portrayed on calendars and postcards, but these lovely scenes still exist out there in every Midwestern state.

Specifically, this scene can be observed in central Wisconsin, "America's Dairyland," as their license plates read. A traveler rolling down state highway #49 can view lovely rural America at many a turn in the winding road, and one of those special turns and scenes includes a wide curve just north of the now tiny village of Scandinavia. Coming around the final bend towards town ushers in the stereotyped image of the countryside at its best. On one side of the road is a tree-lined sylvan lake; on the other side are farmers' fields with red barns in the distance, and on the far horizon flows a small river meandering through quaint-looking stone-arch bridges.

> **Suddenly between the lake and the river there looms on the crest of the rolling landscape a large building that seems strangely out of place.**

Suddenly between the lake and the river there looms on the crest of the rolling landscape a large building that seems strangely out of place. It is a red-brick, three-story building that rises high on the horizon. What is it? Why is it there? A bit of a mystery that requires some history. That odd building once made perfect sense in both its purpose and location; it had its moments and its reasons, even if both are long gone. At one time it put the town on the map, as it were. Amazing to some; confusing to many; amusing to others. Therein lies a tale. . . that requires a little background.

Thumbnail Sketch of Early Scandinavia

When the earliest settlers arrived in the state in the 1830s, they were not permitted to go north to central Wisconsin because the region was still reserved for the Native Americans. (For the first generation of Norwegian immigrants, the area was referred to as Indilandet, Indian Land.)

In 1848, the same year Wisconsin became a state, all that changed with the "Menominee Purchase," an agreement worked out between the U.S. Government and the Native American tribal chiefs whereby settlers could move in while the Native Americans simultaneously moved out of the area.

In 1854, the village of Scandinavia, the first Norwegian settlement north of Winchester, was officially formed by nearly 100% of

Norwegian immigrants. (The same year found the formation of the national Norwegian Lutheran Church in America.) An argument preceded the town's naming, with one strong element wanting to call it "Danger" (pronounced "Dahn-gehr") in memory of Eidanger, Norway, their ancestral home. It was pointed out, however, that Danger in English had a decidedly different connotation and would likely scare away future settlers. Thus a compromise—because there were three "foreign" families in town, namely two Swedes and one Dane—the name Scandinavia was selected as a good choice that still identified the ethnic character of the area's settlers.

The village grew quickly as stores and businesses were built to serve the area farmers. The first industry as such was a kiln for making charcoal from oak logs. By 1900 there were three hotels, two grocery stores (each also sold dry goods), a butcher shop, two blacksmith shops, a wagon and carpentry shop, a bank, post office, barbershop, shoemaker, harness maker, watchmaker, funeral director (who also sold furniture), livery stable, creamery, telephone office, and two restaurants. Most of the above would be found in any frontier community "on the make." Much of the initial start and early growth must be credited to the railroad being there, or as the common line went, "No railroad, no town."

But there were two extra institutions that made the town special. Two miles north of the village stood this huge Lutheran church. It was officially started in 1854 and named the Church of Our Redeemer, though most folks called it The Kross Kirke (Cross Church). It was the first Lutheran church in Waupaca County. The first pastors were from Norway. It was not uncommon to

Norwegian Evangelical Lutheran Church, near Scandinavia, Wisconsin; built in 1862.

have from five to ten baptisms every Sunday; nor was it uncommon to have 75 or more confirmands each spring. The second special reason the town was put on the map: the Scandinavia Lutheran Academy. Initially sponsored by The Cross Church, the Academy, opened in 1893, was essentially a Lutheran high school for young people from all over the Midwest (room and board available; out-of-town students lived on the upper floors). In 1920, two years of college were added and the name changed to Central Wisconsin College.

The Golden Decade

The 1920s were Scandinavia's most prosperous years as an energized, energetic community. Main street itself was paved in 1927. As a service center, the town provided everything necessary for a good and full life. The wide variety of goods and services offered gave credence to the notion that if one could not find what was needed in town, one probably did not need it after all.

Also in the 1920s garages were added to fix old cars or as a place to buy a new one. The population was never higher, approaching 500 citizens. Add to this the numbers attending the Academy/CWC (almost 100 each year) and it was small wonder that the townspeople would bask in its successes and predict even a greater future. It was not to be.

Crossroads for the Cross Church

The initial size of the Church of Our Redeemer was modest (60' by 35' by 15'), but as the congregation kept increasing in size, so, too, did the building. The church was0 added on to again and again and eventually two large wings were added (along with four balconies) so that it could seat 1,200 people. The completed church took on the shape of a large cross and afterwards would regularly be called "The Cross Church" (Kross Kirke). By 1880 it was the largest Norwegian Lutheran church in America in terms of physical size as well the size of the congregation (over 1,500 members).

The first pastor, the Rev. Olaus Duus, came in 1854 and stayed five years before returning to Norway. Apparently he did not think too highly of Americans in general as he wrote in an 1856 letter back home: "America is not Norway; and I think the best cure for discontented Norwegians is to move over here where there is truly so little honesty and authority that one shudders."

In 1888 The Cross Church was the meeting place for the National Convention of the Norwegian Lutheran Church in America, and by then doctrinal divisions were causing arguments and church splits, the primary contentious issue being predestination. The acrimony was so bitter (some 300 angry delegates) during and after this convention that the national church split into different groupings called synods. One local group left The Cross Church in a huff and built a new church in town.

After one generation, the bitterness died down enough so that The Cross Church members and the new church in town members would officially merge again in 1917. Services began to be held every other Sunday in The Cross Church, but because more people lived in town, the country church was less convenient and soon fewer services were held there, going from once a month, to once a quarter; then only twice a year, and by 1925, none at all. This very large structure stood empty long enough for broken windows and snow and rain and pigeons its only occupants.

Church records (not written in English until 1925) indicate their problem of what to do with this "Huge Barn," as one person called it, and finally they voted to dismantle it. The minutes show no opposition to its demise. So in 1928 it was torn down and enough wood came from it to construct two large barns. Today the site is back to farmland, the once important structure there noted only by a small plaque. Among the very few artifacts saved from the church is the baptismal font, now on display in the entrance of the town church. The font showed up in the 1980s in the corner of a grainery on the farm closest to where the great church once stood.

Although perhaps pointless to engage in "what if" dreaming, it still seems reasonable to conclude that if The Cross Church were still there, it would become a "must see" for thousands of ELCA Lutherans, almost a mecca for Norwegian Americans to visit.

The photo shows a portion of the interior of The Cross Church, notably the altar area and the pulpit (note how high up it stands and the steps leading to it). Also of note is the balcony (one of four) behind the pulpit. The small figure seated in the picture is the Rev. Ole Nilsen, who arrived from Norway in 1892 to become the new pastor, a position he held for the next 28 years. Not incidentally, Nilsen was on the Board of Directors of the Scandinavia Academy from 1892 to 1920, and his ongoing dedication to the school earned him the unofficial title of "Mr. Academy."

Inside the church—O. Nilson, Pastor. 1902

Nilsen's daughter, Frieda, after retiring in 1962 from the faculty at Concordia College, Moorhead, MN, wrote about her father, her family and the church in a booklet entitled *Growing Up In The Old Parsonage* (the parsonage was located about 200 yards down the road from the church). Miss Nilsen wrote: "The church building was a commodious frame structure in the shape of a Greek cross. Benches along the walls were used by the confirmands when they came for instruction, and in the middle of the church stood the two big wood-stoves, red-hot in winter and darkly uninteresting in the summer. Each of the four balconies accommodated a goodly number of people, and the big pipe organ in the west balcony, was the only one in a Lutheran church in the whole county.

"Of course women and children occupied pews on one side . . . the men and boys, the other. A huge chandelier [seen in picture] lit by kerosene lamps hung above the middle aisle, as did a handsome ship model, symbolic of the journey of life. [That model ship was saved and is now on display in a glass case in the church in town.] During cold weather, two big stoves in the sanctuary hardly kept anyone comfortable, but one did not expect physical comfort in church."

Catastrophes. First Local, Then National

The Academy building burned to the ground on New Year's Eve, 1919. Within days, the governing board voted to rebuild it on the same location. The decision then was understandable and enthusiastically welcomed, but only a few years later it was regretted as unwise. (The replacement building was/is the red-bricked, three story building noted in the Prologue. At this writing, the building still stands and is used primarily as a storage warehouse.)

The times changed mightily in the 1920s. In education, public high schools had begun their mushroom growth while private, church-sponsored academies were becoming anachronisms. Economically, farm prices would collapse with the start of The Great Depression in 1930. Hard times moved in and stayed for the next ten years.

The Academy/Central Wisconsin College closed in June of 1932, and in September of that year reopened as the Union Free Public High School. The high school closed in 1960 following a merger with the nearby town of Iola. With the closing of the Academy/Central Wisconsin College, and later the high school—and not too long after that the elementary school—the town changed, not for the better. An outmigration of citizens turned a once-thriving community into a shell of its former self. (On a personal note, my father would be the last President of CWC and the first and only supervising principal of the public high school. I wrote a book on these subjects called *The Rise and Demise of Scandinavia Academy and Central Wisconsin College*. Somehow it never made the *New York Times* Best-Seller Lists.)

A Requiem for Schools

Ecclesiastes says that there is a season and a time for every matter under heaven: "There is a time to plant and a time to pluck up what is planted . . ." But nowhere is it written that there is a time for town and country schools to die gracefully; nowhere are liturgies written for these dying schools, dying school buildings, dying towns. Once they showed off a wonderful rural America, one that included a proper education for the children of immigrant-Americans.

Times change, and all those thousands of students who once attended that early Academy, the old high school, the old grade school, are now advanced in years with the large majority already deceased.

Too many rural towns, which for a moment in time broke the spell of loneliness, now themselves stand lonely. Buildings stand empty. Old school buildings stand empty, if they stand at all, monuments to missions completed. Silent witnesses to an era gone by.

And still at this writing, the sense of ethnicity is very strong in Scandinavia. Today most townspeople will first say when asked, that they're Norwegians; not Americans. Perhaps that says something about the importance of belonging to a group. Sure, of course they're patriotic citizens, but there's plenty of loyalties left for their home and their background. "Only in America."

The Scandinavia Academy was one of 75 Norwegian Lutheran Church-sponsored private high schools once common in America at the turn of the 20th century, the Academies lasting until about 1930. Prior to the rise of the public high school movement which started early in the 20th century—and which would be a factor in the later closing of many Academies—church leaders saw Academies as a proper education for the children of Norwegian immigrants. Academies would combine academics, Christian education, and ethnic maintenance all within one institution.

The Scandinavia Academy building (pictured) opened in 1893 with almost 100 students enrolled in grades nine through twelve. The building burned to the ground in 1919 and was replaced by a second building (insert, above) in 1920. Two years of college were added to the curriculum in 1920, and the school was renamed Central Wisconsin College. CWC at first did well, but then came the national economic depression and the school fell on hard times, as did all 75

Academies. The Scandinavia Academy/CWC closed in 1932 but the school reopened that fall as a public high school. By the turn of the 21st century, only one of the original 75 Academies was still operating

Large photo: the Scandinavia Academy, before fire in 1919.
Inset photo: Academy after rebuilding in 1920.

(Oak Grove High School, Fargo, North Dakota); a very few survived by becoming 4-year colleges, (Saint Olaf, Northfield, Minnesota).

Between 1893 and 1932, some 2,200 young men and women attended the Scandinavia Academy and/or Central Wisconsin College before it became a public high school. (The high school would close in 1960, following a merger with nearby Iola; the building since then has become essentially one large storage shed.)

Main Street, Scandinavia, Wisconsin.

Hardware Store Corner

Model T Fords, that once symbol of independence, line the main street of Scandinavia, Wisconsin, on a day sometime in the 1920s, the town's Golden Age. The building on the left with the lettering reads: "HANSON Bros. HARDWARE". At this writing, the letters still remain, even if the corner building is now a deli. At this "Hardware Store Corner," as it was always known, on November 11, 1918, the date The Great War ended, the townspeople gathered for a final "Hang the Kaisar" celebration of the war's ending. A dummy-figure of the Kaisar, a rope around the neck, was hanged from the telephone pole. The dummy was then lowered to street level and set on fire, all this action accompanied by a shouting crowd, firecrackers going off, and guns fired into the air. After all, this was The War to End All Wars. For later generations of young kids—then and now—the "hardware store corner" served as their meeting place prior to starting their day's activities (see later section entitled "A Summer Day").

A Strange Trip

Riding a Tour Bus to See the 'Sites'

The most unique request I ever had to give a talk occurred in the year of Wisconsin's Sesquicentennial (1998), the year state communities were also encouraged to emphasize their own local histories. Among these historically minded towns was my own hometown of Scandinavia (near Stevens Point), which each year puts on a Corn Roast the first weekend of every August.

As part of that special year and celebration, a bus and driver had been hired to take interested persons on an hour-long tour of the area to see the historical sights, and I was asked to present the narration about these places to the bus riders.

The plan seemed simple enough, namely drive around, stopping at different points of historical interest, e.g. the Scandinavia Academy, The Cross Church, the depot, the mill and electric plant, the blacksmith shop, the elementary school, etc., and comment on each place via the bus microphone.

There was a problem with this simple plan, however, namely because there was no Academy, no church, no depot, no mill, no blacksmith shop, no school to see! They were all gone, all razed over the years either by accidents or planning. Hence, there virtually were no "sights," just "sites." A bit of a problem.

See What You Can't See (?)

It appeared that the narration would have to be something like: "Now, folks, observe ahead that broad knoll overlooking the lake in the distance. Imagine standing there a tall, three-story building with a high cupola on top. That's the Scandinavia Lutheran Academy—one of two Norwegian-American Lutheran high schools in the entire state—constructed in 1893. It was an imposing structure indeed . . . ."

Of course this "imposing structure" was long gone, burning to the ground in 1919. Fortunately, the travelers had in their hands an 8" x 10" booklet which included a full-page photograph of the old Academy building. So "turn to page four . . . ."

On to the next site. "And on your right, good people, stood the once-famous Cross Church, at one time the biggest-in-size Norwegian-American Lutheran Church in the entire country; and the largest congregation, too. It could seat 1,200 people!" Alas, by then there was no church to see anymore; we saw just a bare farmer's field. So "turn to page 24 . . . ."

Drive on, Mr. Bus Driver. "There's the depot site. Four passenger trains came and went from there every day of the week. That depot was a hub of community activity." Of course there was no depot to see anymore. Indeed, there were not any tracks left; they had been pulled out, in effect the railroad abandoning this once bustling town. So "turn to page ten . . . ."

> **As one rider said afterwards, "That was a strange trip . . . good thing we had good imaginations."**

This curious situation certainly made for a different kind of historical tour, one in which to see—sort of—the actual sights, one had to turn to the right page in the booklet. As one rider said afterwards, "That was a strange trip . . . good thing we had good imaginations."

Despite these limitations on seeing the "sights," the interest in the tour was high. The bus' first trip left at noon and from then on left every hour on the hour until 6 p.m. Each tour found the bus essentially filled by interested citizens—back home for the Corn Roast in general, but mainly back to see and visit with old friends and neighbors—all giving support to Dorothy's line in *The Wizard of Oz*: "There's no place like home." We try to prove to ourselves that life has a foundation; there's a longing in all of us to go back where we came from. "Turn to page . . . ."

ENVIRONMENTAL DECEPTION

The tour bus filled with Americans rolled along the highway in Norway. This one couple kept noticing a sign on the side of the road that appeared every few miles, the sign reading in big letters:

"FARTSGRENSE" (speed limit).

The confused husband turned to his wife on the seat beside him and asked: "What does it mean?" Without hesitation, she replied straight-faced: "Norwegians are so concerned about air pollution that only in those designated areas are people allowed to pass gas."

He believed her.

Inset: Train crossing over trestle. Large Photo: Scandinavia, WI train depot.

Trains and Depots

Town depots were once a hub of activity. In a time when traveling any distance at all meant going by train, folks could be found at the local depot day and night. It was also the place where the latest news came through via Morse-code and the telegraphy machine, all translated by the important Depot Agent. The depot also became a gathering place for retirees looking for something to do during the days, and they would gather there to visit, along with watching to see who was leaving town and who came in. This picture shows the Scandinavia depot in the 1920s when there were four passenger trains operating daily (note the derby hats worn, which were in style that decade). The town was on the main line of the Green Bay & Western Railroad (went as far west as St. Paul). The inset picture shows a train crossing the trestle over the river in town. Standard fixtures near any depot when there were steam-powered locomotives were a water tower and a round-house (not shown). The mournful but seductive sounds of the steam whistle coming from the big, black, puffing engines caused many a little boy along any railroad line to know what he wanted to be when he grew up: a railroad engineer. And whenever and wherever the trains rolled through, there was always someone to wave to, the brakeman on the last car, the little red caboose.

Demon Aquavit Strikes Again

A note to the uninitiated:

AQUAVIT is a strong alcoholic drink associated with Scandinavians. Pale yellow in color, Aquavit is basically a vodka made from potatoes, with caraway seeds in it to give it its distinctive color and flavor. The Latin word-roots indicate the word means "Water of Life," although drinking too much at one time will quickly lead to a very dizzy life.

Although various brands are available, perhaps the best known is "Linie Aquavit," the label indicating that company production of the same goes back to 1885. Aquavit is often served with fish dinners, and just before the drink is served, the bottle is taken out of the freezer where it has been "chilled" for 24 hours. Thus, when it is poured into a glass, it appears to have the thick fluid consistency of mercury.

An example of the above can be confirmed by the dinner meetings of the St. Paul Torsk Club (they meet once a month to eat torsk/codfish, boiled potatoes and lefse). Just prior to the meal, each person is also served a two-ounce shot of Aquavit, the waiter coming with a bottle taken right out of the freezer. Although warm Aquavit is drunk by some folks, its smell and taste at room temperature is often compared to that of diesel fuel. Enough on Aquavit. It is hoped that this tiny explanation was useful, then.

Dear Svenn:

Well, about this time of the year I usually take a minute to write a few lines to my good firends; the time when I remember all the good things we did together, and indulge myself to the extent of getting a little sentimental.

It is a blustery evening, but here in my den it's cozy and comfy. I am sitting before a nice open fire, typing away, sort of half-listening to an Edvard Grieg tape and slowly sipping an icecold tumbler full of Aquavit. I just wish you were here, and since you are not, the least I can do is to toast your health and happiness, so time out, old friend while I bend my elbow. To you, dear friend! Du er så snill!

I just took time out for another double-snort of Aquavit and while out in the kitchen Ithought of all the time I would waste going backand forth so I just went to the freezer and made up a pittcher of acquavit

Suggested warning label on bottle: AQUAVIT MAY CAUSE ONE TO MAKE MISSTEAKSS

on ice nd brought it in wi th me so I*d have it rightt here besideme and wooulnt waste time runing back andd forthh. So now I)m all sit and so h here goes. Besides that Scandahoovian poontz is a great drink. For som reason it nevver seems to affec me in the slighttast. Can drin k it alldaylong.

The greateest thing tje whoe worrld is griendship. Andbelieve me pal you are the greatets pal anyybody everhad. Do you rember all the well timmes we had together!?: Ezpecialllly that wodderful campint trip. I)ll never forgot the timme yoi put the dead skunnk in my sleepingg bag. he ha Boy how laugheded didn we. Never did get the stin kout of itt. But it wad prety funnay anawayhaha I stil laught about it once in a whille Not as muhc as I used to but whad th heck and after all it waz juss a joke. and if a guy canat have a laff on a good treu freidn once in w hiel wah thehevk.?

Darm putcher is most imptry so i just wentoutand got anoth one an i sure wish you wweer here old freind to heapl me dring ths Aquavit because it are siply deliccius. Parm me while i lif me flfgass to youin good healathth becaus you are the bests pal i had Off cours wh a paul wood do a dirty thnb lick putttinngg a skuunk in a nother pals sleeping bagg. dam if i know. That was a lousi think for anybodyh todo an only a frist class jerk would do it wans't blam bit funey. Stil stinnnkks. An if you thinkinkit sfuney you ar drity lous and werse, a regler drit sekk. Fi Fan! Stilll stinnks. as fare as i%m concered you ca go jumpp in a lak and stya there you drity ratt. So thire.

SnerelyY urs, ,

Kkarl

Oyvind Holt?
He's half Scotch and half water.

The first Scandinavian swing.

The swing as revised by a committee.

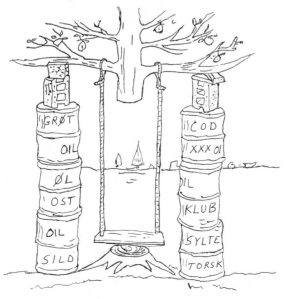

A Summer Day

Really, another nice summer day of school vacation. A day filled with tremendous trifles. All illustrating blissful childhood filled with soft sounds and no fury, signifying nothing special.

Daylight

The sun chins itself on the horizon, but only the folks are awake to witness nature's daily miracle. Not Uncle Øivind, though, who justifies his sleeping in by saying, "If you've seen one sunrise, you've seen 'em all." Uncle Øivind, if he can get away with it, is a late sleeper, even if he is not a little kid like me, lolling there in bed, waiting for his mother to call him for breakfast.

Mom's wake-up call soon comes and the boy's ritual-day is underway. The call is always the same. The same line phrased the same way; no change in cadence nor tempo nor modulation of voice: "*Sett deg opp. Kom og spis*" (Get up. Come and eat)." The message is delivered in a volume just a little louder than a phone call to Aunt Agnes, but not loud enough to be construed as a barking command. My mother is a kind and gentle person. Even awakening her desultory eleven-year-old is a nonthreatening event.

At The Table

The school year menu means either hot oatmeal ("Gotta have sumthin' that sticks to the ribs," says Dad) or hot Ralston ("Let's hear it for Tom Mix!" say I) and a thick slice of wholewheat, homemade bread toasted by first spearing the bread with a long fork and holding it over the open wood fire by removing one of the stove lids on the black Monarch wood-burning cook-stove. Just like an indoor-outdoor campfire with the possibility of blackened, burned toast.

The summer menu is different. It allows the callow lad to eat Wheaties, the cereal his radio hero Jack Armstrong promotes. And besides, eating Wheaties means that when you grow up and get old, like high school age, you will become a great athlete, meaning a great baseball player, the only sport that counts in our town. Maybe become like Joe DiMaggio, even if he does not play for the Cubs. Everybody in our town wants the Cubs to win. Well, maybe not all. A couple of independent showoffs like the White Sox, the team in that rival not-so-important league. Yet the Sox choice is grudgingly acceptable, as long as they are from Chicago, the nearest big city where big-time baseball is played.

Dining Alone

Breakfast is a solitary experience in the summertime. Big brother is up and gone to work on a fox-and-mink ranch just out of town. A smelly job, but it's a job, and the first job he got as a mighty teenager of 14—and by that age kids are expected to go to work. Such are community standards. By 14 get a job! Tough to get old.

The folks of course have been up since daylight and Dad has quickly devoured his slimy, softboiled eggs so that he can rush out to work in his beloved garden. "Gonna be a good tomato year," he keeps telling us. "Great pea crop too, but the beans seem a little slow this summer."

And his youngest son (me) seems a little slow this summer as he dawdles with his Wheaties while paging through the newspaper to absorb the morning funnies, which don't seem as funny as they seem just dumb. (Mr. Dithers should be charged with assault as he continues regularly to kick poor Dagwood in the rumpus.) And to read Captain Marvel (SHAZAM!—whatever that means) seems less appealing in drab newspaper black and white. He's not much better in our big-little-books, either. The Captain needs color, as in comic books, which topic reminds the boy that it's time to trade a stack of comics again with his pal Bergey, which further reminds him he better eat faster as he would be meeting The Berg as always downtown by the hardware store corner at 9:30. (The character Bergey—Lars Bergson—is dealt with more fully as a high school student in Lee's first book about life in a Norwegian-American small town, *The Lutefisk Ghetto*.)

When Mom's back is turned, he picks up the bowl and slurps down the rest of the milk. Mouth wiped with a fast swipe on the back of the hand. Finished. Time to roll.

Away For The Day

Running out the front door and riding off on your bicycle requires no explanations, no goodbyes in the summertime. Also no parental reminders, no warnings. What's there to warn you about? They know you're going off to meet up with your pals and play—play something, do something—all within the confines of the village, or at most the township (sometimes we ride our bikes out of town to go swimming at Sand Lake). Parents know you'll be peddling back home again for lunch immediately after the fire siren blows each day at 12 o'clock noon. And besides, what can you get away with? The whole town is watching you! Every citizen is an undeputized constable. (Many years later we came to appreciate the fact that the whole town did watch over us.) They watch you from their wood-frame houses, where every house has a front porch, the place to sit at the end of a summer day and watch the world stroll by—or whiz by if they're cars.

So the only reminder comes from yourself to make sure that before you hop on your bike that hanging on the handle bars will be the two required items for the day, any summer day: a baseball glove and a swimming suit, the latter grabbed off the sagging clothesline where it has hung all night to dry. (Electric dryers are not yet invented in 1941.) But no towels to go with the swimsuit. Towels are for sissies.

Eleven is a pretty good age. Pretty much a carefree age, too. You're old enough to be given limited responsibilities but never so many that you can't have lots of time to play. You sleep well all night long. You're old enough so that the little first and second graders think you're old, and the big kids in junior high think you're little and too young to get beat up. And mothers are always asking you if you'd like some ice cream and lemonade.

Peers and Jeers

Kids' clothes, even for ding-a-ling Depression kids like us, require the wearing of something proper—a term used very loosely in this context—meaning that other kids will make fun of you if what you wear strays too far from the acceptable norm. And a mighty simple norm it is, which means you wear overalls (anyone who calls them blue jeans is putting on airs), but not the bib kind; bib overalls are for hick farm kids. And don't wear a belt, either! If your pants are just a little big, well, just pull 'em up. If your pants are way too big, you pull in your gut, pull two belt-loops together and wedge a stick in between, and then your pants fit real tight.

As for wearing shorts, even on the hottest of sweltering August days, Never! Don't even think about it. You'll get laughed at all the way back home to your mother. Among our callow crowd, the term shorts mean underwear. Period. Only ginky kids from the city, who show up briefly when forced to visit their rural relatives, wear shorts, often fancy ones to match their Arrow shirts. As to our shirts? They're usually hand-me-downs and are one step away from the rag-bag hanging in the backroom closet; and some days you dig into the rag-bag to retrieve your favorite. As long as your shirt has at least one button, it's O.K. And besides, these nondescript items of apparel come off as soon as the sun gets high in the sky, at which point the shirt joins the suit and glove on the handle bars.

Oh, as for shoes? None. Barefoot time. In the summer shoes are for Sundays only. Shoes don't go back on daily until school starts up again the day after Labor Day. Oops, one more requirement: put nothing on your head. Mothers' pleas of guaranteed heat strokes notwithstanding, you go bareheaded. And sweat. And burn. Endure it. Caps and hats are only for old people. Result: by September 1st, every kid in town is brown as a nut as well as a sunbaked blond.

An Assembly, of Sorts

Our gangly gang gathers at the hardware store corner on mainstreet each morning. Well, actually assembling just off mainstreet street, meeting around the hardware store corner where the seldom-used horse-hitching rail stands next to the red-brick store. Each biker (Hell's Cherubims?) comes careening in, slams on the brakes and skids appropriately in a half circle to a stop. While waiting for the rest to career in, we ride in small circles, glump around, fiddle around, horse around. Eventually the riders all stop and end up with one foot on the ground and the other leg thrown over the bike bar. We think we look cool that way. To the parade of hardworking farmers going in and out of the hardware store beside us, we probably look to them exactly like what we are: a bunch of pint-sized and lazy town kids trying to figure out how to fritter away another day without making it seem too much like frittering.

There are no community organized activities for the kids in the summers or any other season. Never heard of such a thing. Kids devise their own daily activities, even if they don't exactly know what that big word means, which is why we gather by the hardware store in the mornings: to figure out some group activities to do and when to do it, like when we should start the softball game for the day? Big decisions. It's sort of ancient Greek pure democracy at work (11 a.m. is the agreed upon starting time for softball), after which solemn determinations (yesterday, we agreed to spear suckers at 10 a.m.), the plenary session of the kid-congress adjourns, and its members ride off to parts unknown, all members heading out in pairs.

"Three's a crowd; four is a mob," or so the saying goes. We know that two-at-a-time works the best. We know nothing of psychology and never heard of group dynamics but only know that when there's three of you, you end up arguing and can't get much done and usually one rides off in a huff, leaving the other two with some parting words they learned from their big brothers.

Following a Loose Agenda

Bergey and I decide to start the day with anticipatory hope #1: Going to see what the bums are doing down by the depot. We know they never do nuthin'; but that doesn't stop us from hoping. This destination first requires riding to the top of a hill overlooking the railroad yard and when getting close, sneaking through the high grass behind Karl Knutson's sagging house—a house he bought from a Sears-Roebuck catalog and had assembled. We then crawl on our bellies to the very brink of the hill before peering over and down at the bum-shack below, maybe a hundred yards away.

The bum-shack is a single abandoned freight car with the wheels removed, the shabby shelter dragged away from the tracks where it half stands, half leans against the tall water tower. We've never gone inside the shack because we're always too scared, convinced we'll be strangled by some deranged transient who hates little kids. (We believe every bum is John Dillinger in disguise.) But from the distance at which we observe them, the hoboes look just right—exciting, dangerous.

This day, however, is like every other day. We see a couple bums still sleeping outside under some newspapers; two others sitting on a log in front of a smoky bonfire, each with an opened can of something in his hands as they dine on their somethings. One man called out something to somebody inside the shack and someone calls back something but we don't understand either something. Boring. Time to leave and do something else. Maybe tomorrow will be better.

> **But from the distance at which we observe them, the hoboes look just right—exciting, dangerous.**

To the Millpond

Time to go back to the center of town and check on how the fishing is going in the spillway waters below the millpond dam just off mainstreet. Although the dam survived, its original function as a power-producer and turner of millstones for the local community ended in the late 1920s when a large utility company bought it out from the

Anderson family and closed it down. (That phrasing is something like chopping a tree down and then cutting it up.) The once tall, wooden structure over the grinding mill-wheels and the turning turbines—the Power House building itself—had been demolished and carted off to the dump, leaving only an empty open area with little reminder of what once was. The only reason to go there any more was for the fishing in the river just below the spillway. Upon arrival, we spy one fisherman at work/at play. Fishing being a term that has implied goals as to its possibilities and outcomes, there is a proper way to ask a fisherman of the results, namely "How-ya-doin'?"

Seeing old Kristoffer Hanssen sitting there on the high cement section over where the water came through from the pond behind him, our expected question requires a small variation, namely "Catchin' any-thing?" Actually we have already peeked into his five-gallon milk pail and seen exactly how he is doing, noting two still-swimming bluegills, one fat pumpkinseed, and one dead snake pickerel. Hence comes

Kris' expected reply, "Purdy gewd, den." Even this limited conversation requires high volume voices because of the loud noise from the crashing waters at the bottom of the spillway. "Whatcha usin'?" is the next code phrase perfectly understood even if we perfectly understand what baits he is putting on his fishhook by observing in his Hills Bros. coffee can some skinny angleworms wriggling on top of the dirt and a dented minnow bucket with about a half dozen shiners in it, half with their white bellies up:

> "Ahh, den, yus' vorms 'n minnerss, den."
>
> "Well, good luck. Gotta go. See ya, Mr. Hanssen."
>
> "Ja-ja, bye den, *gutter* (boys)."

Killing Time 'Till Gametime

Still about a half hour until the softball game starts. What to do in the meantime?

"Whaja wanna do now?"

"Dunno. What do you want to do?"

"Let's check out the pickle station."

"Good idea." (It will get checked anyway at some point in the day. So when we go is the only variation in the agenda.)

The pickle station lay on the other side of the millpond and area farmers come there daily—sometimes twice a day at the height of the season in August—with their freshly picked cucumbers and sell them to the station manager, a weasel-faced little gnome of a figure referred to by all the locals as simply "Pickle Paul." Paul buys, and in turn Paul sells the cukes to a big buyer with whom he had a contract as a supplier, a company called Jewett & Sherman.

The appeal for kids to include the pickle station on their daily route is two-fold: 1) absorb those powerful pungent smells of the thousands of cucumbers as they lay piled high in tall, wire-covered bins in the storage sheds, and 2) observe Pickle Paul in his attempts to best (read: cheat) every farmer in each financial transaction. His operation is summed up by the men in front of the barbershop who call Paul's buyer not by their name of Jewett & Sherman but by a politically incorrect variation of their names.

So who today will be the intended victim? Alas, we arrive too late and miss him as the last "john" is just chugging down and out the long gravel driveway in his makeshift "pickup." It is Lars Trulson in his car-tractor, the latter term given to the vehicles of farmers who take a cutting torch to a regular sedan car and chop off the entire auto frame behind the front seat, thus quickly converting a car into a small truck, of sorts. It may not be pretty but it works, sort of. Cheap, too.

We ride directly to the sheds and suck in those great aromas! Almost intoxicating in their powers. Hmmmmmmm, wonderful! Paul sees us but never says hi, hum, hell or high water. He is not much for conversation anytime, certainly not with dopey kids.

We left. Destination/s: the grade school softball field (can't call it a diamond; too many misplaced big trees and large rocks in the field for that designation; it's more like a rectangular wooded cow-pasture, minus the cows). But on the way we plan our stops: first stop at the workbench in Jackob Gjerseth's garage, followed by a slow non-stop cruise past Turkey Torgerson's melon patch. Each has its value.

Expecting the Expected

Our bikes fly through the wide-open front door of the garage, our tires barely missing the outstretched skinny legs of Jackob himself who is lying under a Hudson and swearing—in Norwegian—at the rear transmission about four inches from his big nose. He then adds a line in English aimed at a slipping crescent wrench: "Damn knuckle-buster!"

Although Jackob can see only rotating wheels from his perspective, he never says a word, being more than used to bikes coming and going all day long, each kid there for the same reason, i.e. squirting some oil on some moving bike parts that received a stream of oil whether needed or not. Jackob fills the oil can each morning.

Helping a Heinous Heist

Out the garage, fast-peddling through the back door, hurrying past the blacksmith shop, hoping the blacksmith won't spy us (he scares the liver out of us!), hurrying on to the last house on the east edge of town, the place where homes end and farm fields start, to observe the vast garden planted alongside the road by Turkey Torgerson. (His nickname comes from his enlarged Adam's apple, plus his sagging jowls and loose neckskin that all in all make Mr. T. look like he is about ready for a Thanksgiving oven.)

Our mission at this spot is to "case the joint" for our older brothers, and in this "case" determine exactly where the rows of Turkey's fat watermelons lay in relation to the road, and hence the degree of time that would be required to steal some and race quickly with them to the open trunk of a waiting car. With this exciting task in mind, we idle our bikes by slowly, slowly one way, gawking and mentally measuring felonious opportunities for the green-and-black stripers that would be ripe by month's end. Then we turn around and ride slowly, slowly back again, all the time pretending to be so engrossed in the flora and fauna in the ditches as to be mesmerized by their beauty, even when the dirty, quack-grass-covered ditch reveal only two dirty Blatz beer bottles, a tossed-out diaper, and a flattened can of Sir Walter Raleigh pipe tobacco. As to the success of the planned caper? A piece of cake, we can report. So, mission accomplished. Time to play ball.

A Pickup Pickerupper

The gathering for the softball game has a goodly number—about a dozen kids—all there on time. Being on time has filtered down from our Norwegian American parents and this touch of carry-over culture approaches cleanliness in its nearness to godliness. The ritual of choosing up sides begins at 11:02, just after the semi-hidden bat and ball are pulled from their hiding place in the culvert next to the six-holer outdoor biffy by the grade school building. Now to form the teams. Picking sides is a lesson in humility as one awaits his name being called by one of two (for the day) agreed-upon captains, and if you are picked absolutely last, it is a lesson in degradation. Though Stink (alias Mousebrain) Olson was so bad,  so totally uncoordinated (he doesn't really run, he sort of flops forward) that he has gotten used to this daily booby prize. To put it charitably, neither Stink's body nor his heart is in the game. He is always placed in right field, the area where the batted balls will least go, and even if a rare fly ball headed his way, he is normally too busy studying the cloud formations in the sky to pay any attention to any dumb ballgame.

Hardly ever are there enough kids for two full teams, which leads to some players being responsible for playing at least two positions, e.g. the deep fielding shortstop also plays left field while the third baseman also kind of plays shortstop. With no umpire, the only way to strike out is to swing and miss three times, so essentially each kid at the plate eventually hits the ball at some point and heads for first base, which location is marked with a gunnysack partially filled with sawdust. Second base is a 10-inch-long two-by-six; third base is a flattened carton that once held a six-pack of Miller High Life beer.

The entire arrangement—entirely applied pragmatism—for the contests has led to some high scoring games (yesterday the score ended 83 to 57) because there is no limit on the number of innings played. The game is officially terminated when the town fire siren blows its one lone, lingering, ear-piercing sound at high noon, at which moment the game ends abruptly forthwith, with all team members stopping immediately and heading for their bikes, to peddle furiously homeward for lunch.

That Long Wait Before Swimming

Whereas departure in the morning involved no parental "be carefuls," the after-lunch dismissal brings forth daily the same strident parental admonition of "Don't you dare go in swimming until you've waited at least an hour after eating." We kids all hear the same words, or close variations thereof. The portentous warning, if violated, means: if you jump in the lake right after eating, you will for sure get stomach cramps for sure, and thus drown for sure. No doubt about it. For sure. Because no one ever tests this hypothesis, it must be for sure true.

The fact that there are no lifeguards didn't seem to bother the adults. Nor are there admonitions about swimming all the way across the lake, a half-hour physical venture that is a true test of flotation endurance. Then, of course, swimming back again to the beach requires even greater endurance. Yet there are no adult warnings regarding this truly dangerous practice. (Not to swim across the lake, when asked by one of the guys, brands anyone a chicken!) All parental cluckings, however, deal only with eating and then swimming too soon afterwards. Stomach cramps and your demise. Guaranteed. For sure.

To the Barbershop Bench

The one hour interim between dining and bathing finds many of us kids back downtown sitting around, but never on, the long wooden bench in front of the barbershop, the spot where the oldtimers (anyone over 40) gather each day about 1:30 after waking up from their midday naps. The men who come there really like each other, but each man would rather pass a kidney stone than admit as much.

This fondness for each other's company, however, does not apply to "newcomers," who are essentially defined as anyone who moved to town less than 20 years ago. Strangers are not to be trusted. New residents have to prove up their claims, which proof is not accepted until the second generation emerged.

At these barbershop gatherings we put into practice the rubric, "Don't speak unless spoken to," and seldom is part two of that sentence initiated. So we sit on the hard cement, listening and watching, learning the learning of adults, like learning the Norwegian American 11th Commandment: "Avoid all confrontations." At least while the offending opponent is still sitting there. This is the citadel of passive-aggressiveness. The social construct of benign amiability leads to some mighty boring conversations, there being no end to what can be said about the weather with its multitude of themes and variations. Regardless, one should not start an argument; it makes everyone nervous to have any trouble-maker in their presence. However, after the alleged offender gets up and leaves, then they can start picking apart both the man and any or all of his foolish notions, e.g. "Dat dum'-cluck Korn Ferden ain't got da brains of a schicken, den. Goofier den a _____-house rat. Dis FDR New Deal stuff iss nonsense, den. Maybe Communist, tew! President Franklin Deficit Rosenfeldt, den."

The real insult to an area citizen is being pronounced a "Tomorrow Farmer." They're the worst kind, the person who never gets around to doing what he's supposed to do today, but maintains he'll get around to it "tomorrow."

Amid character assassinations are regular folk philosophy, as when Hans Rasmussen observed: "Yeah, den, money can't buy happiness, but it shewer kin get ya da kind of misery dat's easier to put up wit'."

Meanwhile, time crawls on, thankfully. Finally the hour wait is over and it's time for the daily jump in the lake.

To the Lake

Silver Lake lies on the edge of the town. Not a particularly interesting name nor lake. Given its physical features, it could just as well be called Round Lake, and thus might achieve an even less interesting title. The shallow lake (20 feet at its deepest point) means that during long and frigid winters, it will not provide the gamefish with enough oxygen and thus the fish "freeze out," as the phrasing goes. We witness hordes of belly-upped northerns and bass washed along the shoreline in spring when the ice goes out. But those tough bullheads survive!

Almost the entire lake is surrounded by farm fields with pastures going right down to the water's edge, so sometimes there are more cows in the lake than swimmers. On the town side lies the small swimming beach, owned not by the town but by a local farmer (Peter Peterson, whose immigrant father was Peder Pederson) who allows swimming there. He also allowed two bath houses to be built, a project of the town's Booster Club, the one and only civic organization organized to support the community via limited programs and projects.

The girls' and boys' bath houses are about 100 feet from each other, the latter useable although stinky and unsanitary inside, with a strong odor of urine from its too-frequent-use as a lavatory (most of the boys went in the lake). The girls' changing house at least does not smell bad, but does have some extra holes in the boards made by high school boys wrenching out the knots in the lumber so that they can peek at the girls when they are dressing/undressing. There is limited success for the peeping-toms, however, because almost all the girls both arrive and depart wearing their swimming suits. Can't win 'em all.

A none-too-sturdy dock runs out from the shore about 50 feet into the lake. No diving boards, no rafts, no slides, no nothing; just the dock. "Getting wet" when the gang is there was not a delicate wade-in, not a one foot forward at a time slow procedure. Only sissies do it that way. The cultural "law" means that as soon as you hurriedly get your suit on ("Last one in is a rotten egg!"), you hustle to the dock and run wide open to the end and yell "Geronimo!" before diving into the water. Even if the coldness of the water guarantees your lips to turn blue in five minutes, that is the only way to get wet. But we enjoy it. At least we tell ourselves at the time that we are having fun, even if we aren't.

Finally Free Time

Those hours after swimming and before supper at the rigid hour of 5:00 (whether hungry or not, you eat at 5:00!) allow for boys' individual tastes and choices of activities. Lots of 'em. Among the favorites is gopher-hunting, often called "drowning gophers," a procedure that calls for pouring water by the buckets-full down gopher holes, and when the soaked critter comes up and out from the hole, hitting it with a baseball bat. Actually, this alleged sport, of sorts, pays! Cut off the gopher tail, take it to the County Court House, and collect ten cents for each tail.

Another money-maker, of even more limited rewards, is scavenging the town dump for empty pop bottles. Bring the empties to the grocery store and get a penny for each bottle!

A non-income event is going to the co-op with your BB gun and shooting sparrows. This is regarded as a civic contribution, there being no love for sparrows or starlings or blackbirds. Just don't shoot any robins!

Another post-swimming venture of dubious moral quality is "cooning" apples. One did not steal them (that is wrong) but "cooning" them is somehow O.K. Either way, it is a common way to hold off hunger pangs until supper is on the table.

Then there is reading. One does not announce to the rest of the gang that he was going home to read. That statement would not be well received. Not that reading is bad in itself because every kid is expected to know how to read. To be viewed as illiterate is a clear sign that any such a dumb-head can expect to spend appropriate time in the corner of the schoolroom, sitting there on a stool with a Dunce Cap on his head. You gotta learn to read! If for no other reason than not to be viewed as a moron.

But the idea of reading just for fun, let alone to learn something, is a questionable activity. Outside of comic books, which are entirely acceptable among our peers, reading is something you only do in school. Period. Reading is not to be fun; it is work, assigned work! When summer vacation comes at last, you are free from reading for three months! With that common understanding, summer reading for kids becomes a solitary, clandestine affair. And maybe that is what adds to its excitement. The appeal of the forbidden. Thus Tom Sawyer and Huck and the Mother West Wind book series await the curious. Ahhh, the thrill of anticipation in starting a new book. To love reading—and let nobody know about your crime.

> **Ahhh, the thrill of anticipation in starting a new book. To love reading—and let nobody know about your crime.**

But the Days Dwindle Down . . .

The sun sets earlier each day. Windows recently opened to let in the cool air are now closed to keep in the warm air. September looms, the month that comes too soon, and yet comes in the nick of time. In time to save us from ourselves who are getting bored with the summer days' rituals, but of course would never admit as much. All those things to look forward to in May have been done too many times by August. School is looking better all the time, although never spoken.

There's a twinge of energy that surges forward each September that comes to the youngest first graders or the oldest grandparents who, with a whiff of nostalgia, can still remember their own starts of yet another school year in Days-Gone-By-Too-Fast. Nothing like the sight of that first Back To School newspaper advertisement to remind all that the start of a New Year has less to do with the official calendar than the start of a New School Year.

September feels like spiral notebooks, sharp pencils and stiff new shoes. Labor Day produces sounds of the teacher's officious voice on that first morning of roll-taking; squeaky chalk scribbles on blackboards; and best of all, recess, and the happy screams of children on the playground. September brings forth smells of brand new overalls, varnished floors and noon-hour smells of opened brown paper sacks and the odors that waft out when the lids come off of Karo Syrup lunch pails.

The "New Year" is about to start; the summer days are about to end. Summer vacation is over, but can Christmas vacation be that far away? No, it just seems that way at the time.

LARS: "I wonder what that Kirkby boy will be when he graduates from college?"

TRULS: "About 35."

Some Basic BASICS in Norwegian:
A Few Phrases Readers May Find Helpful

God dag.
(Goo daag)

"Good day." Hello/Hi.

God morgen.
(Goo morn)

"Good morning."

God aften.
(Goo aft-in)

"Good evening."

Hvordan har du det?
(Vordan har do dey?)

"How are you?"

Bare bra, takk.
(Bah-re brah, tahk)

"Quite good, thanks."

Snakker De Norsk?
(Snukker Dee Norsk?)

"Do you talk Norwegian?"

Ja, litt.
(Yah, leet.)

"Yes, a little."

Nei, desverre.
(Nay, des-verreh)

"No, unfortunately."

Jeg kommer fra Amerika. "I come from America."
(Yay kom-er fra Amerika.)

Snakker du engelsk?   "Do you speak English?"
(Snukker do engelsk?)

Vær så god.   "Here you are."/"Come and eat."
(Ver sheh goo.)   (literally Truly so good.)

Takk for maten.   "Thanks for the food."
(Tahk for maht-en.)

Det var bra.   "That was good."
(Dey var brah.)

Ha det bra.   "Goodbye."
(Hah dey brah.)   (literally Have it good.)

God natt.   "Good night."
(Goo natt.)

A Special Year

A SPECIAL CELEBRATION

To celebrate the centennial of the first boatload of Norwegian immigrants to America in 1825, the planning committee arranged to rent the Minnesota State Fairgrounds for a grand four-day celebration, June 6–9, 1925.

Over 100,000 people came to the St. Paul fairgrounds for a variety of events ranging from pageants to ball games to concerts to bygdelag conventions to worship services. They heard many speeches, notably one from the President of the United States, Calvin Coolidge, who had agreed to attend the celebration.

By 1925, some 850,000 people had emigrated from Norway to America, with the largest number of them settling in the states of the Upper Midwest. Although this figure represented only 1% of the total U.S. population, their influence was significant in several areas, notably politics, as indicated by the fact that in 1925 the governors of Minnesota, Wisconsin, North Dakota, South Dakota and Montana all had Norwegian backgrounds.

Yet things had changed remarkably for this ethnic group by 1925. The most important factor in maintaining heritage—language—had already dropped off dramatically. Almost all the speeches given at the celebration were given in English; almost all of the program/brochure was printed in English.

The most symbolic event at this centennial celebration was recog-

50

nized when 500 Norwegian American children, wearing red, white and blue capes, formed a living Norwegian flag. Then they reversed their capes to transform themselves into an American flag. No one missed the message: In 100 years, these Scandinavian immigrants had assimilated into an American world.

Following the celebration came two significant outcomes to maintain and promote their heritage:

1. the formation of the Norwegian American Historical Association (NAHA), headquartered at St. Olaf College, Northfield, MN, and

2. the formation of Vesterheim (Western Home), The Norwegian American Historical Museum, located in Decorah, IA, and connected to Luther College in Decorah.

Statement made by a complaining parishioner in 1925 to his Pastor who had the gall to give a sermon in English:

"I have nothing against the English language. I use it myself every day. But if we don't teach our children Norwegian, what will they do when they get to heaven?"

Vi Har Det Godt i Amerika

(WE HAVE IT GOOD IN AMERICA)

How routinely was *Vi Har Det Godt i Amerika* stated by thousands of Norwegian Americans after 1825 when they first began their massive —for Norway—immigration to America. Eventually over 850,000 would emigrate, a figure approaching one-third of their entire population at that time!

How routinely did their offspring, the first and second generation born in the U.S., hear those words from their immigrant parents and grandparents.

And how routinely has the line been forgotten—and more likely not even heard—by later generations. Time for another reminder.

Speculation:

Was the phrase *Vi Har Det Godt i Amerika* usually mumbled or proclaimed? Announced proudly or grudgingly? How many listeners took issue with the statement? Or was it a common knowledge assertion to which an audience merely nodded agreement?

Even when stated positively, what might have been their definition of good? Certainly for almost all who spoke the line, good would most likely be compared to the lives they left behind in the old country. Some lines from Amerika-Letters (letters sent back to Norway) suggest some answers to the above questions:

"Here (in America) it is not asked what or who was your father, but the question is, what are you?"

Or . . .

"Farmers and artisans are just as good as merchants and officials."

Or . . .

"The clergy is not regarded, nor indeed regards itself, as better than the common people."

Many Scandinavian American readers of sufficient vintage may remember both the time and the circumstances when they first heard a Norwegian-American immigrant utter that statement. I clearly remember the time and the event when I first heard the words—indeed, heard it many times in one afternoon—and yet when heard did not really understand its full meaning and implications. My excuse? I was only a child of seven, but even then I was impressed because those speakers (my grandfather and his siblings) so sincerely meant what they said.

The Scene

A fenced-in lawn, overlooking a barnyard, on a small 80-acre farm located about 12 miles outside of Decorah, Iowa. A sunny, warm summer day, the kind of gentle, lazy Sunday afternoon that was perfect for an outside, family picnic-dinner. Wooden folding chairs, borrowed from the nearby Lutheran church, had been hauled in and set up on the newly cut grass, the now fragrant lawn mowed with an iron-wheeled push lawn mower. The chair arrangement seemed scattered haphazardly except for four chairs placed in a small circle in the shade near the fat trunk of a tall, hulking willow tree. The four chairs were

Appreciation for our country—in part summed up in the word patriotism—has historically affected the nation's citizens deepest and widest and fastest during wartime. However, that same appreciation came for immigrant groups coming to America; it just took a little longer.

for four special people, all immigrants.

The sounds and smells coming from the open summer kitchen door revealed both the workers who were in full motion preparing the outdoor meal as well as their main entrée for the gathering—chicken, fresh chicken, the near-by hen house occupants reduced in numbers just that morning. Moving, chatting, laughing women in their print dresses bustled their way back and forth from the kitchen carrying heavy food-laden trays to the long, sturdy tables placed in the shade alongside the white, wooden-framed, square farmhouse.

> **They did not want to hear any more news about that crazy little man in Germany, the one with the silly moustache, the one who was taking up too much air time.**

All the ingredients necessary for a delicious summer spread were filling up the space on the sagging tables, and all the many foods there were homemade, all except the jello—good, red, jiggling Lutheran jello—with whipped cream on top and sliced bananas on top of the whipped cream.

Someone yelled for the radio to be turned off, partly to save the batteries and partly because they did not want to hear any more news about that crazy little man in Germany, the one with the silly moustache, the one who was taking up too much air time. Besides, his name was synonymous with trouble, even war. But that European mess was none of our business.

The Guests Arrive

Rolling down the long driveway, the tires crunching the white limestone gravel, came some dozen automobiles. Their occupants would be on time for the picnic. Norwegian-Americans are on time for everything. Cleanliness may be next to godliness, but being on time was somewhere in that equation. The procession was led by the late Knute Lee's '37 Studebaker driven by his adult son, Knute Jr. or *Lille* (little) Knute, as he was called, compared to his dad, *Stor* (big) Knute, who had only recently passed away. The car behind Knute's was brother Ole Lee and a bulging carful of his extended family, all crunched into a '34 Dodge, the smaller grandkids sitting on laps, their heads bumping the roof. Next came Agrim Lee in the spiffiest auto of the day, a new, two-toned DeSoto, while in vehicle-contrast was their sister Ingeborg and her husband Halvor in their old Chevy pickup, the truck bed filled with a raft of their grandkids, ready *barna* (children) eager to jump out and run and play with eager cousins soon surrounding them. None of the immigrant brothers nor the sister drove cars anymore; they were all too old.

The above vehicles and more (i.e. more relatives' cars), parked side by side in a mowed hayfield across from the front gate of the farm owned by their brother Lars, my grandfather. Even before coming to a full stop, some occupants jumped out: big kids, little kids, big sisters, smart alecky brothers. Trailing behind the kids came their clucking mothers and harried fathers, several of the latter now free to reach for their snoose boxes. Amid the confusion of talking and yelling and rushing bodies and squirrely kids, there were plenty of *Takk for sists* (essentially "good to see you again") among the grownups, along with their cries and threats to settle down hollered at unlistening young-uns racing towards the machine shed, the corn crib, the barn, all seeking future hide-and-seek destinations. The extended family count totaled about 50.

Before long the men, who within five minutes had congregated, seemed to find it necessary to take a stroll down to the horsebarn for some reason or other. They never said why. A few of them made several trips back and forth before the meal was ready and those who lingered in the barn the longest returned to the yard speaking louder than the rest and laughing more, too. Their breath also smelled strange. All confusing to the youngsters, half-observing curious adult behavior and manners.

Time to Eat

When at last came the welcome call of *Vær Så God* (essentially "time to eat"), the hungry horde crowded toward the makeshift buffet, forming a queue, waiting impatiently and watching the three men and one woman meandering slowly, carefully to the four chairs in a circle. Their meals would be brought to them. The "special four" were not only the special guests but also the reason why the rest of the people could or would be there. They were the four who emigrated before the turn of the 20th century, coming one at a time, the older ones later helping the younger ones travel *til Amerika*, and leaving behind one sister and one brother who chose to remain in Norway. (A fifth immigrant brother, David—along with aforementioned Knute Sr.—had died several years before.)

Collectively the six siblings, originally from Lærdal, Norway, were the parents, grandparents and great-grandparents of the jabbering progeny surrounding them, the hungry families waiting to load up their plates. Quantum reproduction, the Depression notwithstanding.

By this year, 1938, the special four had all aged visibly. Their walk was slow, their eyesight dimming, their hearing diminished. The men whose once muscular frames filled out their bib overalls and work shirts to button-popping pressures now found their Sunday white shirts hanging loosely from shrinking bodies and stooped frames. Two brothers wore suspenders, not for fashion or show, but simply to hold up their baggy pants.

These three men and one woman were, of course, my grandfather Lars, my great-uncles and one great-aunt. Although they were very elderly and somewhat feeble (within five years, all four would be deceased), that day they were one happy quartet. They laughed a lot; they ate a lot, and the men slurped their hot coffee from their shaking saucers, giving both coffee and food an extra straining through walrus mustaches. And of course they talked only in Norwegian. Their new world just seemed better understood and appreciated in their first language; the jokes were funnier, too.

I was seven years old at the time. My cousins and I had run around and had no problems as long as we adhered to the parental admonition of "Don't get in anybody's way." During these runs, darting by those oldsters in a circle, I would first hear the line, *Vi Har Det Godt i Amerika*. Even a seven-year-old could translate that line. Had it been heard only one time, it would have been immediately forgotten, but in the course of the afternoon the sentence became commonplace, so much so that I finally stopped beside them to try to assess the situation, wondering why they believed they had it so good.

What's So Good About It?

Didn't seem so good to me. Indeed, spending summers on Grandpa's farm was a step backward in time, a trip back to the primitive. The big farmhouse with the cupola on top had no electricity and no inside plumbing. Drinking water came from a hand pump standing just outside the kitchen door. The toilet was a two-holer just down the hill, the front entrance covered by vines and hollyhocks. Toilet paper was the Sears-Roebuck catalog, unless we were lucky and Grandma had bought a crate of carefully-wrapped peaches. As to needed household heating? A black, wood-burning Monarch range in the kitchen, wood-burning space heaters in the living and dining room, and no heat whatsoever for the upstairs, a palpable problem in the winters. And the farm so isolated. Although only 12 miles from town, it might have been 1,000 miles as we hardly ever went there anyway. Grandpa

> **"No other country except Ireland contributed so large a proportion of its population to the settlement of North America"** as did Norway.
> —Harvard Encyclopedia

Lars had no auto and maybe it was just as well as he didn't know how to drive a car, just his horse and buggy.

Yet there that day Lars sat so obviously happy, sipping on a glass of cold grape nectar, smoking his smelly pipe, fanning himself with a folded *Decorah Posten* and joining the chorus in their lively discussion in which someone some time would again maintain with full assurance, *Vi Har Det Godt i Amerika.*

Did they have it so good? With the exception of the brother Agrim, who was a tailor in town (however, he owned a farm, which he rented out), the others were farmers, and they all owned their farms. Therein lies not only a clue but the entire explanation: They owned, mortgage free, their own farms, owned their own land! Only in

America. Freedom, opportunity and equality reigned, giving humanity a better way of life and a greater hope for the future. They knew it; they experienced it. For them owning a farm was their monumental accomplishment, considering the situation back in Norway.

When one learns that only 3% of Norway is arable, that the average farm size even by the year 2000 is 11 acres, that for literally centuries Norwegian farm-families lived generation upon generation as perpetual tenants, peasant non-land-owners who barely survived the hardness and harshness of the climate, eking out an existence in the category of *husmenn/cotters/crofters* (all three are the same), no wonder the oldsters used the phrase so often. Whatever term used, they represented the bottom of the economic barrel: peasant farmers. Even by mid-19th century, the chance of ever owning a farm for oneself in Norway—unless one were the oldest son and thus the only inheritor—was virtually impossible.

Let the formal wording in the Harvard Encyclopedia state their case:
> *"The emigration movement in Norway may in part be seen as an important aspect of the self-asserting emancipation of the peasant class." (p. 752)*

Four self-asserting peasant immigrants—now landowners, free and independent yeoman farmers—sitting outside on the lawn that hot August day left not only a foreign country, but escaped poverty and a way of life that had seemed permanently established. They were a tiny part of a migration that shook "the order of unchangeableness" to its foundation. Their day finally came when they could and would and should say with total understanding what their grandchildren and great-grandchildren take for granted: *Vi Har Det Godt i Amerika*. They did. We do. Because they had made it so for us.

Norsk Wisdom

Borte bra; hjemme best.
(Going is good; home is best.)

Ingen er for gammel til å lære.
(No one is too old to learn.)

Når enden er god er alting godt.
(All's well that ends well.)

Penger spart er penger tjent.
(Money saved is money earned.)

Alt som glimrer er ikke gull.
(All that glitters is not gold.)

Øst, vest—hjemme er best.
(East, west—home is best.)

Barna er fattigmanns rikdom.
(Children are the poor man's riches.)

Det nytter ikke å gråte over spilt melk.
(No use crying over spilled milk.)

Hver sin lyst.
(To each his own desires.)

Om hundre år er allting glemt.
(In 100 years, everything is forgotten.)

Perverse Pleasures for Young and Old

It may seem perverse if not perverted, but one of the activities we as kids chose to do on weekends was to go downtown after dark and loll around across the street from the only two taverns in town and watch the goings-on. In other words, we went there to watch the drunks.

How this form of youthful entertainment is to be interpreted, I know not. I only know that things could and would and did get so boring that just for something to do, we'd ride our bikes to town and once there took a sense of delight in simply standing around looking across the street at inebriated men walking and/or staggering back and forth on main street as they went from one tavern to the other and back again.

Our gallery included both genders. Several of the girls in our gang seemed to get as much a kick out these unsober spectacles as the boys. We would sit there and watch, and of course make snarky and smart-alecky remarks to each other. The boys did it as much to impress the girls as to add any useful commentary. The boys interpreted their quirky statements as witty. Some of the girls interpreted those same remarks as half-witted.

Friday was a good night for these drunk-shows as it was payday. Indeed, the common line expressed at the time for any received paycheck was "Payday On The Railroad." And for some, payday was the time to hang one on! And we watched them hang themselves, as it were.

It does not take much to amuse the simple mind. Our being there was a testimony to that aphorism. Sometimes it did not take much alcohol to affect some simple drinkers, like "Two-Beer Torvold Tollefson" who, as the men who sat on the bench in front of the barbershop said of him sarcastically, "Dat guy can't hold his liquor, den." That was no compliment. Conversely, "holding your liquor" was a compliment.

As stated, we kids made steady editorial snipes regarding those pie-eyed figures on exhibition. After all, we knew all of them and watched them well enough so that we could make comparative notes as to how their performances varied over a single summer. For an extreme example, Peder Prestegaard was a rather restrained-in-manner drunk in June but by late August he'd lurch forth from the not-wide-enough tavern doorway to walk directly to the side of the street and then and there nonchalantly pee on main street. If at the moment he apparently had it in for one of his compatriots back at the bar, Peder would single out that man's vehicle and pee on it.

Oh, this was great fun to watch! Or so we said to ourselves—until this one night when it ceased to have any more appeal; it became less a comedy than tragedy. And an awakening.

It began when Johannes Einarson emerged from the tavern, one floppy shirt tail hanging out and over his fat stomach and sagging pants. He was taking tiny baby steps forward, then stopping, then taking big steps backward. Little forward progress being made. Anders Holten blurted out that the only way Johannes would get to where he wanted to go was to turn around and head the other way.

Nobody laughed. Nobody said anything. Our mouths were closed and our stomachs had tightened, because there in our witnessing group was Johannes' daughter, Marit. A bad situation. Embarrassing. Unnerving. What do we do? What do we say? Pretend you don't see him? Pretend you don't hear his off-key singing, his bellowing out "Red River Valley"? Suddenly it seemed like a good time to be someplace else, anywhere else.

Marit saved us by saying loudly, "Boy oh boy, is my old man gonna catch it when he gets home tonight! Ma will crown him with a frying pan and he'll wake up in the morning with a lump on his head as big as his big red nose." And then she laughed.

And then we could laugh. Saved. Then someone could add, "Don't think *The Grand Ole Opry* is ready for your pa." "Ha ha." And another: "Maybe he could get hired by the Arrow Shirt Company." "Har har." And another: "Nah, he'll make bigger bucks as a two-step belly-dancer at the Stork Club." "Har de har har."

Marit came back with the line, "Good thing the weekend is coming up. He can't hide from Ma tomorrow. Wow! Will our woodpile get bigger in size by tomorrow night! And the silent treatment for him will last a week. Big bag-o'-wind can't stand it when he can't talk to somebody. Ohhh, but it will be fun . . ." And she laughed again.

And that seemed to end the problem. She was O.K.; it was O.K. Or so it seemed. By then "Skunky Skurvik" (so nick-named for his regularly being drunk as a skunk, even if no one had ever seen a drunk skunk) staggered out, and his appearance was worth a dozen snipes from most of us, all except Marit who said nothing. She sat in silence.

The 10 o'clock hour was approaching fast, the time of night when the "You be home by 10 o'clock . . . Or Else!" parental warning was remembered and we all got ready to leave. Suddenly the wind came up strong as we said our banal good-byes, and it was then that a wind-blown streetlight started swinging back and forth and its light briefly caught the face of Marit, revealing her moist eyes and the tears running down her cheeks. She tried to say a strong good-bye of her own but it wasn't there. She knew; we knew. Drunkenness is not funny. It was time to grow up.

The guys.

A Guy Thing

The guys shown returning from doing a "guy thing"—that is spearing suckers in the local river, an annual spring ritual. Ancient photo (1949) has ancient car ('32 Studebaker) and a quartet of then teenagers: (1. to r.) Gene Moe, Art Lee, Marvin Erickson, and Roger Bergman. All have been mentioned in Lee's books, although their names were altered, with Bergman—"Bergey"—the featured character in *The Lutefisk Ghetto.*

Owning A Single Shot .22

A RIGHT OF PASSAGE IN RURAL AMERICA
AND A FATHER WHO SAID "NO"

Growing up to become—or not become—a hunter in an upper Midwest country town depends primarily on one of two influences: your father or your friends. If either or neither wanted a rifle or a shotgun of their own, then the likelihood of your ever buying a hunting license was minimal.

If I were to follow my father's views, I would never have owned a rifle. Indeed, would never have fired a single round. Dad did not like guns of any kind; he had none around the house. He had his reasons—very good reasons as it would be revealed years later—but he never explained them when I was a kid. Just his simple, succinct line more muttered then pronounced was all he would say. "I don't like guns." (His idea of "arms protection" in our home was to keep a baseball bat in his clothes closet.)

But my friends liked guns. More significantly, they owned their own guns. Ah, the power of peers. Owning a rifle was more than a sign of maturity; it was practically being a grown-up. A proper ritual along maturity road; as good as eighth-grade graduation and even better than church confirmation! Just think of it, having a rifle of your very own! The type of firearm most wanted was a single-shot, bolt-action .22 Springfield rifle, the kind in which you raised the bolt, pulled the bolt back, inserted a tiny .22 shell into the chamber, closed the bolt into a locked position, then cocked the gun by pulling back on the end piece mechanism. When that back part clicked in, the gun was cocked and ready to fire.

Rats and Cans and Bottles

The town dump, about a half-mile from the village, became a favorite spot for my pals and their .22 rifles. There they hoped to shoot rats but if there were no rats showing forth, there was no end to the numbers of bottles and cans waiting to be plinked by a .22. At this location the guys let me shoot their guns all I wanted, providing I brought along my own shells. (An indication of the year this occurred is suggested by the price of the shells at that time: 22 cents for .22 shorts; a box of long-rifle shells cost a whole quarter.)

From the point of view of the State Conservation Department and the license bureau issuing hunting licenses (for $1.00), one could legally hunt at age 12. When I finally reached that advanced age, I hoped my father was running out of excuses, as well as getting just plain tired of all the begging and yowling he had to put up with.

However, ongoing pleas for owning my own rifle ("But everybody else has got one!") remained unheeded. These negations of my stern father had started out as a firm "No," and/or "You're too young," but persistence and "old age," along with a little whining and a lot of pleading eventually led to "Maybe, we'll see" to a plain "Maybe" to at last, "Well, gotta check with your mother first."

A. O. Lee.

Then a trump card showed up: I had learned of an available used rifle for sale from a retired farmer, Louie Leppen, who lived across from the church. Mr. Leppen had moved into town from the farm and figured he didn't need the gun anymore and was willing to part with it for ten dollars.

(I had that amount saved. No small feat when your weekly allowance was a dollar.)

Success At Last!

Finally, grudging consent came from the lips of the naysayer. That was a red-letter day! A wonderful day! An unforgettable day! When the final "Well, O.K." came from his pursed lips, I left the house immediately, this time walking and not taking my bicycle for fear that I might drop the magic prize on the way home if I were riding a bike. (Although this historic event would at this writing fit into the category of ancient-history, I can remember that day as vividly as if it happened this morning. Some events are like that.)

A Twist To the Tale

Upon my return home with my dream cradled in my arms, my father met me at the door and announced sternly that I was never to shoot that rifle until I received proper training about guns as well as guidance in gun-handling and hunting-safety. And he would be the instructor!

The shock of that announcement did not exceed the shock that followed. He knew all about guns! He sat me down and in an hour's time explained the difference between rim-fire and center-fired cartridges. He talked about muzzle-power and rifling; he noted the importance of trajectory and velocity; the difference between automatics and semi-automatics; the advantage of pump-action over bolt-action; he emphasized proper grain-size/bullet-weights and mushroom-bullets versus hollow-points. I was impressed; I was amazed!

With a yardstick as a prop, he even showed the proper way to aim. One takes aim by starting with the gun barrel pointed up toward the sky and brought down to eye level; not start by pointing down and bringing it up. Only fools and city-people (same thing) did it that way.

That afternoon, a cold, gray, September day, we drove to the countryside and stopped at a low spot where a creek ran between two hillsides. The spot was deliberately chosen for target practice. There was no one around; there were no farm animals around, either. He emphasized the mandatory need to know who or what might be in the vicinity where one would be hunting. And one must carefully select the background where your bullets would fly so as not to have any houses or barns in the line of fire, let alone people. He also explained the dangers of ricocheting bullets that could glance off and hit something unwanted, which is why we were to practice our shooting into the side of a hill. And "Never NEVER point your rifle at anything you do not want to shoot!"

Then the Moment of . . . Youthful Shock

At last the time came for the first shot to be fired. A tin can was placed on the ground in front of a stump at a distance of some 25 yards. At that point the gun came out of the gun case; at that point my father came out of his old self. Total shock. He was not the stone-faced figure always in control, always in command of his own feelings, his own visage. He was not, at that moment,p/ the always commanding supervising principal of the local high school. He seemed to be losing it. When he first touched the gun and then held it in both hands, he began to sweat on this cold autumn day. He was breathing hard, almost panting. The color in his face alternated from white to red and back again. As he held the rifle, his hands were visibly shaking. He seemed to have come unglued. For a 12-year-old lad watching, this was a father he had never seen before—nor would ever see again. He could not believe it, let alone understand it. (The explanation would come years later when the son reached his own adulthood.)

After about a minute of this confusion and uncertainty, however, the father regained control of himself again and the actual shooting practice went forward without further shakes or facial color changes. He returned to his old self; from then on the ongoing firing of the rifle proceeded uneventfully and turned out just fine. It was a special day. That day was never forgotten. Now I could go hunting with my friends.

The Explanation, of Sorts, of Fatherly Fears

One learns about one's parents in stages. On this road to understanding, one hears a lot of information about the folks that is not recorded in the head; for whatever reasons, it does not stick. Too young, too immature; too self-absorbed. At the time the parental info seems at best irrelevant. Even in elementary school I sort of knew that my dad had once been in the U.S. Army. Any more than that I was not interested in. By junior high I had learned that he was a soldier in World War I, The Great War as it was called then. Still not properly impressed. After all, he was not Sergeant York. By my senior high years it came out that he was in the infantry and served on the Western Front the final months of the war. Things were changing; my interest was growing more and more. Then in college I finally began at last to understand his military background and combat experiences and asked him personal and pointed questions, questions he at first tried to duck: "I don't want to think about it, let alone talk about it."

Little by little it came out of him that he had served as a combat foot-soldier in three major campaign attacks on the front lines on the Western Front. That he was lucky to be alive. He learned fast that he had two pieces of equipment that would and did save his life several times: his gas mask and his rifle with a bayonet attached. He told me combat is horrible beyond words, and hand-to-hand combat is the most horrible of all. And actual gun and artillery battles are loud and confusing, with earthshaking cannons going off around you, shrieking incoming artillery shells landing in your vicinity, shrapnel flying, men

A. O. Lee in uniform.

yelling and wounded horses screaming in the distance. He said that in combat you fight in those moments not so much for your country as for your buddies around you, the guys you depend on for survival each day and who depend on you; the young men you see get shot and killed almost daily. He said that to avoid the word "killed," he and his buddies used the term "went west." Thus so-and-so didn't die, he "went west." Too many of his close friends in the mud and blood of the trenches "went west." In summation, he would firmly state that he had seen enough of killing, and fired enough rifle shells to last him ten lifetimes. When The Great War ended he hoped he would never have to touch a rifle again.

How It Never Ended

In the last years of his life, he would mention the war only on one day, one date: November 11th. In many way the happiest day of his life; the day The Great War ended. And he would remember every detail of that morning when he was hunkering down in a water-filled trench bordering no-man's-land in France when 11 a.m. came (the 11th hour of the 11th day of the 11th month, 1918). He vividly remembered seeing his First Sergeant running and bobbing along the line, all the time yelling those wonderful words: "Cease fire! Cease fire! The war is over! The war is over!"

The most wonderful words for millions: the war is over. But it was not really over for those soldiers who were there. Even if their lives were spared, they were invisibly scarred forever. New terms would be devised later to generalize the mental scars for combat troops severely affected by their war experiences. After World War II and the Korean War many combat troops returning home were declared "shell-shocked." The Viet Nam War and the post-Gulf War wordsmiths came up with "post-traumatic stress disorders."

For The Great War troops there was no nomenclature applied for their mental sufferings. Nor were there any official efforts to ease their pains. Their problems were just supposed to sort of go away in time and be completely forgotten. And perhaps that was true for many of the troops. I had thought that was the case for my father, but it turned out not to be the case.

Delusions

His last years were spent in a nursing home. He was a few months short of his 90th birthday when I again went to visit him. By then he was in a wheelchair; by then he was at times confused and disoriented. At times he believed he was back on the Western Front. That day I visited he kept calling out to his army buddies to run for cover because another German cannon shell was coming. He yelled that he could hear its screaming path and it would be landing close! He then wondered out loud if he had enough ammunition packs on his belt because he was firing so many rifle rounds. He next hollered a warning to a perceived machine-gun crew to stop firing because their gun-barrel was starting to get red-hot. The war—his war—was there that day, some 65 years after it had officially ended.

> He vividly remembered seeing his First Sergeant running and bobbing along the line, all the time yelling those wonderful words, "Cease fire! Cease fire! The war is over! The war is over!"

A minute later, however, he was again lucid and back to the present world.

He would die two weeks later.

Small wonder then that the father did not want his 12-year-old kid to have a .22 rifle.

BB Gun Tag

Here are two young boys at the age when rural kids wanted to own a gun of their own, a single-shot .22 Winchester rifle. Picture of author (on right) and his brother Bob, shown all duded up and ready for church. Bob—Robert E. Lee, red-haired and freckled-faced—was a musician; he would much later direct the Wartburg College Band (Waverly, IA) for nearly 40 years before retiring in 1995.

At their age (in photo) each owned a Daisy air rifle, called a "BB gun". An indica-

Robert E. Lee, left and author Art Lee.

tion of their youthful sense, or lack thereof, might be revealed in their participating in the then common boys' game of "BB Gun Tag" (3 pairs of overalls worn), a combination of Hide-and-Seek and Quasi-Marksmanship. While all would go off and hide, the boy who was currently "it" would—after closing his eyes and counting out loud to 100—go off to find someone hiding, and when found, aim his BB-gun and shoot him in the rear end. (Rules said no shooting above the waist.) The receiver of the stinging BB was then "it," and the game continued until all participants had at least once received the dubious honor of getting hit and becoming "it." For this activity there is a proper adjective spelled almost the same in English and Norwegian: dum.

CLEAR SIGNS YOU'RE FROM THE NORTH-COUNTRY

You don't complain about the weather, you just dress accordingly.

You take secret pleasure when your state takes the dubious honor of being the coldest spot in the nation.

Someone in the store offers you assistance and they don't work there.

Your local Dairy Queen is closed from November through March.

You know winter is less a season than a way of life.

Jumper cables make an acceptable wedding gift.

You understand that your sewer system will freeze if there's not enough winter snow.

You have apologized to a telemarketer.

You've heard of lutefisk and lefse but may not have eaten either one—but you know someone who has.

You believe ice-fishing is a form of mental illness.

You believe that ice-fishing has saved more marriages than counseling.

You consider it a sport to gather your food by drilling through 20 inches of ice and sitting there all day hoping your supper will swim by.

Kids fool their younger friends by talking them into putting their tongues against an iron post in January.

You can go out into your back yard in April and clean up after your dog with a 7-iron.

You grew up believing that rice is only for dessert.

Any supper is greatly improved when preceded by a bump-and-a-beer.

In May it is necessary to use both the car's heater and the air-conditioner on the same day.

All the brave—if naive—folks who plant their gardens before Memorial Day know they're pushing their luck.

The first time you saw *Grumpy Old Men*, you thought it was a documentary.

You're sure the hardness of the butter is inversely proportional to the softness of the bread.

"Boughten bread" is a sign of sloth in the kitchen.

You've also been told that "the early bird gets the worm" but you know it's the second mouse that gets the cheese, and you get tired of having to explain the second-mouse bit.

There's something about the North Country that grows on you. Perhaps it's the amazing varieties and even the harshness of the seasons. People love the extremes, even as they complain, and they take pride in the fact that they can weather the weather.

Tall Tales of the Great Indoorsman

Growing up in rural America, where nature rules the day, and where weather is the main topic of the day, there was a special nature-related statement laid on a very few. It was one simple complimentary line: "He's a real outdoorsman."

That was a great compliment, an accolade suggesting a virtuous, rugged looking figure who was husky and athletic; who was both an active sportsman and a true conservationist. A Real Outdoorsman of course hunted and fished, but also jogged and skied and naturally supported the town baseball team by working on the ball diamond. Also a Real Outdoorsman worked diligently to build up wildlife habitat, improve trout streams, cut brush for ski trails, and help the Conservation Department stock fry in the area lakes and streams. A worker. A doer. A goer. A hero of sorts.

And whatever a Real Outdoorsman might be doing at the time, he always looked the part. His attire was a kind of uniform-for-the-occasion. It may be uncertainty about how we appear in the eyes of others that leads us to slip into whatever uniforms our occupation or conditions dictate. The axiom goes that we are what we eat; it should also be added that we are what we wear. Rebels or conformists, we all wear uniforms, as it were. A Real Outdoorsman wears . . . well, what a Real Outdoorsman is expected to wear. Depends on the season.

There was another local line that also got laid on a very few, but this line was not positive. It was a pejorative for the truly undeserving, namely "He's a real indoorsman." This line was applied to those who pretended to be outdoorsmen, but seldom fired a shotgun, wetted a line, strapped on a pair of snowshoes or threw a baseball, let alone help in reforestation or restocking or doing any useful activity that required work. Mesmerized by this whole outdoorsy business, they were wanna-bes pretending to be one of the anointed. Posers. Phonies. The call of the not so wild.

The Call of the Not So Wild

The leading figure in this second category was one Donald Blegen who, at this writing, is long gone to the Great Outdoors in the Sky, but he is not forgotten.

"Don-Man the Con-Man," as he was known behind his back, was actually a decent enough fellow. He did not cheat anyone, he did not steal; he did lie, but the only one semi-hurt by his lies was himself. His title came from his trying to con folks into believing that he was a Real Outdoorsman when he wasn't. He did not even like being out-doors; he much preferred being indoors where he could loll in warm comfort, tell whoppers, and drink beer. Lotza beer.

Had Don-Man just not blabbed on and on about his alleged outdoor adventures, folks would have paid him no 'tention. However, he loved to relate dreamed-up "Me and Joe" stories, as illustrated:

"Me and Joe wuz crawlin' through this thick grain field jus' before dawn and we could hear them honkers babblin' away in the slough below us and it was tough scoochin' along on my belly what with Ol' Betsy—my 10-gauge double-barrel—weighin' half a ton and me losin' sight of Joe though I could hear him moaning when he rolled on some sharp rocks but we wuz set to get ourselves a couple of geese no mat-ter how tough it wuz so we wuz gonna sneak up on 'em, and even though it was colder than a mother-in-law's kiss, we wuz sweatin' like hogs . . . jeez, we work like crazy . . . ."

Maybe his fanciful stories could have been partly ignored ("Joe" was a made-up cousin) had he not at the same time tried to look the part. Don dressed—he overdressed—like a Real Outdoorsman, but what he wore was always at least one season off. Folks could tell what the real season was/wasn't by checking Don's attire and then jumping ahead (sometimes backward) at least three months. Don planned it that way. Dumb, maybe, but dumb like a fox.

In the summers he wore a tan duck-cap and a camouflage hunting vest over a brown flannel shirt, the vest slots filled with shotgun shells. On a long leather cord around his neck hung two duck calls, one for mallards and one for bluebills. Unless it was a sweltering hot July day, Don donned hip boots, rolled down below his knees, allowing him to swagger in noisily into the local bars, boots flapping, where he would try to tell the guys returning from the fishing lakes and streams that what he really loved was duck hunting and that he just couldn't stand the waiting for fall to come.

> **When fall came, Don had switched to wearing a porkpie hat with so many fishing flies stuck on it that the hat was hard to pick out underneath.**

When fall came, Don had switched to wearing a porkpie hat with so many fishing flies stuck on it that the hat was hard to pick out underneath. Again there was a vest but one with an array of small pockets that held little boxes filled with enough fishing tackle to supply a bass store. Around his neck was an elastic cord and attached to the stretch-cord was an Orvis brand trout net. If he could find anyone to listen to him (he often bribed listening ears with free beer), he would inform him that fly-fishing for rainbow trout was the greatest of all outdoor sports and he couldn't stand the waiting for the season to arrive.

His get-up was a deliberate move not only to enhance his alleged image but also it allowed him to stay indoors and drink beer while at the same time denigrating the current sporting season as unworthy of outdoor activity. (That's like having your beer and drinking it too.)

Yet his living and dressing for the wrong sporting season had its problems. Often in the wintertime, when the temp was near zero and the wind chill factor at minus 25, Don hustled into the bars wearing only a baseball cap and a light baseball jacket . . ."and couldn't stand the waiting for the season to come."

A Real Phony

Yes, he was a phony but he was such a real phony as to make the whole thing a happy joke. It was entertaining. Some bar patrons could hardly wait for his arrival in his inappropriate costume. He was a welcomed actor. And the patrons were kind of actors, too, in that no one said anything negative about his costumes. After all, ours was a look-the-other-way culture of smiling and laughing and joshing; of compromise and conciliation, where it was considered bad form to say exactly what you think. Besides, we need eccentrics. So no one confronted him, let alone accused him of either fraud or stupidity. If the guy wanted to dress in goofy ways, well, let him. He thought he was in uniform when really he was in costume.

Don apparently could not make that distinction. Uniforms ask to be taken seriously. Uniforms have meaning because they help define not merely who their wearers are but what they themselves believe they are. The dark business suit is as much a uniform as the blue uniform worn by a police officer; both kinds of uniforms suggest competence and authority. A costume suggests frivolity, inauthenticity and theatricality, and Don's ill-timed get-ups represented all three of the latter.

So Don was tolerated. And besides, he added some comic relief. After all, he didn't harm anybody, even if at the same time he didn't fool anybody either. Great theater. And he obviously loved what he thought he was doing, or not doing, whatever the case. A Real Indoorsman in Outdoorsman's Clothing. Takes all kinds.

As to his final reward? Who but the friends of Don-Man would at his funeral slip secretly into his coffin a 12-pack of Bud wrapped with a leather cord with a duck call attached. It was January. Proper timing. An Indoor/Outdoorsman to the end.

Immigrant/Emigrant Music

One definition of Folk Music:
 Songs written by folks who never heard of copyright laws.

One aspect of ethnic music is the faithfulness with which it reflects trends and episodes in the saga of emigration, immigration and assimilation. For example, lyrics tell of Scandinavian immigrants who sought fortunes in gold mining in the West, in lumberjacking in the Upper Midwest as well as the Pacific Northwest, of farming the flat Red River Valley, of labor unrest in the mines of Michigan, Wisconsin and Minnesota, and more.

There are satirical songs on failed dreams in general and one specifically on the failed colony of New Norway, centered about the town of Oleana in Pennsylvania. Famous violinist Ole Bull stunned his countrymen when in 1850 he bought, or thought he bought, 120,000 acres in Potter County for Norsk settlement. It was a magnificent scheme, Bull believed, but ended in magnificent failure in three years. Among the reactions to this "dream" was poking fun at the whole goofy project with a rollicking ballad sung for two generations on both sides of the Atlantic. With some 25 verses, it was called simply "Oleanna." (See next page)

Oleanna

Verse 1
Oh, to be in Oleanna,
that's where I'd rather like to be,
than to be in Norway,
and drag the chains of slavery.

Refrain:
Ole-Oleanna, Ole-Oleanna,
Ole-Ole-Ole-Ole, Ole-Oleanna.

Verse 2
In Oleanna land is free,
the wheat and corn just plant themselves,
then grow a good four feet a day
while on your back you rest yourself.

Verse 3
Beer as sweet as Munch'ner
springs from the ground and flows away,
and cows all like to milk themselves,
and the hens lay eggs ten times a day.

Verse 4
And little roasted piggies
rush about the city streets,
inquiring so politely
if a slice of ham you'd like to eat.

Verse 5
So if you really want to live,
to Oleanna you must go,
the poorest wretch in Norway
becomes like a king in a year or so.

Vers 1
I Oleanna,
der er det godt å være,
i Norge vil jeg ikke leng're
slavelenken bære.

Refreng:
Ole-Oleanna, Ole-Oleanna,
Ole-Ole-Ole-Ole, Ole-Oleanna.

Vers 2
I Oleanna
der får man jord for intet,
av jorden vokser kornet,
og det går så svint det.

Vers 3
Og bayer øl så godt
som han Ytteborg kan brygge,
det risler i bekkene
til fattigmannens hygge.

Vers 4
Og brunstekte griser,
de løper om så flinke,
og forespør seg høflig
om noen vil ha skinke.

Vers 5
Ja, reis til Oleanna,
så skal du vel leve,
den fattigste stymper
herover er greve.

Folk Music

All immigrant groups to the U.S.A.—there were 106 of them—arrived with their own folk songs, their own musical styles. Later American music would be influenced by some of these imported varieties.

All groups had their own folk songs and religious music as well as their dances. There were basic characteristics of all folk music; notably it was:

1. by/for the common people;
2. not written down initially;
3. often "applied" music for certain occasions, such as holidays, wedding parties, birthdays, lullabies, dances and the like;
4. regularly accompanied by an instrument, often a violin.

Folk music could be instrumental or vocal or both. Although used primarily to entertain each other, in the old-old days (pre-1900) there were folk music "Calls," that is, vocal calling to faraway farm animals to lure them back home. Also there were calls to folks on the other side of the mountain—it was called "La-La Singing"—to communicate back and forth. (Today they use cell phones.)

Illustrations of different ethnic groups' folk music would include Polish polkas, Irish jigs, Scottish airs, British ballads, German lieder, Austrian waltzes, Latin American and African rhythms, Scandinavian mazurkas, and more. To all of the above can be added special instrumentation connected with each. (Bad Norwegian joke: A distinctive Norwegian violin is the Hardanger Fiddle; it has eight strings, not the usual four. Thus while a normal fiddle requires catgut, the Hardanger Fiddle requires the whole cat. Uff da.)

Ballads

In contrast to folk music, there were dozens of ballads written in the Scandinavian countries and these ballads were essentially commercial music; they were written to be sold (as sheet-music). Ballads also reflected the times, episodes, hopes and fears of emigration as ballads "tell a story."

There were hundreds of stories to tell and these fell into different categories. Understandably there were many "Farewell Songs" written.

When the lyrics were positive, they were named "El Dorado" songs (sometimes with tongue in cheek), which predicted the riches that would soon be theirs in the New World. On the opposite end were "Disaster Songs" about emigrant ships sinking, burials at sea, and hunger and malnutrition for those sailing steerage class. And even if the ships arrived, "Disillusionment Songs" portrayed America as a dangerous destiny.

"Religious Freedom" ballads were especially popular in Sweden, based on the fact that 19th century Sweden then had the most repressive religious laws. Denmark turned out to be the country in which American Mormon missionaries had their greatest conversion successes, thus producing both pro and anti-Mormon lyrics.

"Economic Hardship," the major factor in Scandinavian emigration, had many songs with different interpretations, especially in Norway, which in the 19th century was the poorest of the Scandinavian countries. Some lyrics state bitterly that desperation hardship forced them out when they did not really want to leave. Yet other musical scores predicted that hardship would end once they arrived in their *Vesterheim*, their Western home.

Closely related to hardship were "Class Society" songs along with "Proletarian Music," which placed blame on the stratified societies from which they were fleeing. However, a few writers were more optimistic about this class thing, and told stories in musical form about how the immigrants would soon get much money and return to where they belonged, their Scandinavian homeland. A few extended this success story to the point where they would become so rich that they would return and buy their own farms and join the landed gentry.

Still—and alas overall—the ballads written had a theme of sadness, the basic assumption was that hundreds of thousands of their fellow countrymen were leaving their homelands, never to be seen again; sometimes never to be heard from again. These attitudes in musical form led to another category, "Reunification in Heaven" ballads.

Fortunately, amid all this downer music, there were plenty of songs that were just plain fun; the aforementioned "Oleana" being a good illustration. And then, of course, there was "Nikolina."

Fun For the Vocally Impaired, the Musically Retarded

Funny folk songs had appeal to Scandinavians in America, and one of those songs would at the turn of the 20th century make any Nordic Hit Parade list: it was "Nikolina." As to the song, it contains the three most necessary ingredients for success:

1. a catchy melody;
2. singable notes;
3. amusing lyrics.

Even the "can't-carry-a-tune-in-a-bushel-basket" non musicians would sing "Nikolina" with gusto. No real Scandinavian party could end without one rousing rendition of "Nikolina." After all, everyone knew the music and the words.

As to the lyrics? Well, perhaps it is most seemly to suggest that they can fall into the category of "beauty being in the eye of the beholder." The lines are hardly the poetry of Bjornstjerne Bjornson, who wrote the lyrics for the Norwegian

> **No real Scandinavian party could end without one rousing rendition of "Nikolina."**

National Anthem (*Ja Vi Elsker Dette Landet*) which in terms of high/low notes is as difficult to sing as the American anthem. It's just as well that the composer of "Nikolina" remain properly anonymous. "Nikolina" was once popular in Scandinavian communities everywhere in America, and there was no more-Scandinavian community to be found in 1900 than Minneapolis.

Snoose Boulevard

By 1890, Minneapolis had replaced Chicago as the principal destination of Scandinavian immigrants. In absolute numbers, by 1910 there were 16,145 foreign-born Norwegians in Minneapolis, and there were even more Swedes! Writer Lincoln Steffens in 1903 declared

Minneapolis the second-largest Scandinavian city in the world, and added that the city was "A Yankee with a round Puritan head, an open prairie heart, and a great big Scandinavian body."

Add the Danes, Finns and Icelanders to the Twin Cities population and it is little wonder that certain sections and streets received both official and unofficial Scandinavian names (e.g. Cedar Avenue became "Snoose Boulevard" because of much consumption of snuff, called snoose by its Scandinavian residents). This development was hastened by the establishment of the Scandia Bank in 1883 on the corner of Cedar and 4th Street.

The many Scandinavian businesses on Snoose Boulevard included saloons, the owners getting and keeping their customers by providing entertainment such as ethnic singers and comedians. Few in these categories had more appeal than one Hjalmar Peterson who took as a stage name Ole Skrutholdt. Ole could tell jokes and he could sing and the climax of his act came with his rendition (in Swedish) of "Nikolina." Only then was the crowd fulfilled; only then could they go home satisfied.

Unfortunately, in time Skrutholdt became a victim of his own stubborn ethnicity (Norwegians claim that the term "Stubborn Swede" is a redundancy). Too soon a new American-born generation of young men came to the saloons (women would not be caught DEAD in a saloon!), and because they could not understand the Swedish lyrics of "Nikolina," they demanded Ole sing it in English. No way. Ole would not budge. Keep it pure; it loses something in translation. And so a generation gap would change the saloon business, but not as much as the 18th amendment, which officially closed all American saloons from 1920 to 1933.

Later musicians would, of course, continue including "Nikolina" in their repertoires, notably two popular Twin Cities bands that continued their successes into the 1950s. One was Ted Johnson and His Scandinavian-American Recording Orchestra, and the other Thorstein Skarning and His Norwegian Hillbillies Band. (To update, "Nikolina" is in 2004 still available on the albums of Leroy Larson and His Scandinavian Ensemble, a Twin Cities group.)

To readers who have never heard nor heard of "Nikolina," here at least—and at last—are the words, *på Engelsk* (in English). Enjoy!

Nikolina

1. When you're in love you're in an awful torture,
   whoever's tried it will not disagree.
   I was so very fond of Nikolina,
   and Nikolina just as fond of me.

2. I asked her father for her hand in marriage
   and got the answer in the strangest way.
   I never yet got out on any doorstep
   in such a hurry as I did that day.

3. So I went home and wrote to Nikolina,
   "Oh, Nikolina, won't you meet me soon!
   Please meet me in the woods on Wednesday evening,
   and be there with the rising of the moon."

4. And there I met a figure disconcerting,
   the moon no greater glory could attain.
   The one I met was Nikolina's papa,
   armed with the meanest, most disturbing cane.

5. And then my knees, how they began to tremble.
   I tried to run, but did not have a chance,
   for in the woods, as on my knees I stumbled,
   the cane began to do a polka dance.

6. Then I went home and wrote to Nikolina,
   "There's not the slightest bit of hope in me.
   If you don't end me of this awful torture,
   I'll end it all by jumping in the sea."

7. Then Nikolina answered in a hurry,
   "Oh, darling Ole, don't be so unwise!
   A suicide is nothing but a dumbbell.
   Why don't we wait until the old man dies?"

8. And so I wait, and so does Nikolina,
   to see the old man kick the bucket soon,
   and on his grave we're planting in remembrance
   the cane he used upon me 'neath the moon.

Dancers in the Community Hall, Scandinavia, WI.

Ol' Time Dance to Ol' Time Music (1950s)

Compared to the popular dancing styles of young people in the 21st century, the above photo shows very different (read: old) ways of dancing, i.e. couples touched, and sort of held each other; discreetly, of course. Whether Ol' Time or not, women then often danced together (men did not) for a most practical reason: there were not enough men available for dance partners. (On the far right is a tall, skinny guy in sweater; he's the author dancing with Judy Jorgensen, his future wife.)

Rightly named, the Community Hall literally and regularly brought the community together as an all-purpose gathering spot for social events year-round. From dances, basketball games, plays and box-socials to Christmas programs, rollerskating, oyster-stew suppers and whist tournaments, the hall welcomed everyone. (For a picture of the outside of the hall, see *Leftover Lutefisk*, page 233.)

A Tale of the Country Mus and the City Mus

(ACTUALLY NOT MICE, JUST LODGES)

The old saw that "life is a struggle" can also be applied to Sons of Norway lodges. They struggle. Just to keep an organization going each year is the ultimate in success, regardless if each and every office can be filled (and if each is filled, and if each officer comes to the lodge meeting, there will be a pretty good crowd there that night.)

It is a positive sign indeed if there is a lodge election where there is a choice of candidates for officer positions. 'Tis not always easy to fill the election slate with even one person.

Age-ism is the major problem in continuing a lodge year after year. It is the elderly who make up the major membership in most lodges, and always, but always there is the goal to get younger people to join.

Even defining "younger" is hardly agreed upon. Although a bit of exaggeration is allowed in this illustration it makes for a good story: Two members of different lodges were talking at a convention and one asked the average age of the membership in the other's lodge. The person replied, "103." He followed this number by announcing that he was "only 69," and thus the rest of the members called him "Sonny."

An added concern for many if not most rural lodges is financial. Too many are forced to limp along on a shoe string budget, and on occasion the really dedicated members must reach into their own pockets—and pocketbooks—to bail out the bunch and eke the struggling organization into the black at the end of the fiscal year. Tough to be a

Country Mouse and survive.

On the other end is the rich City Mouse. Though perhaps in the minority, there are still some very well-off Sons of Norway lodges. And a few are not only well-off, but rich! The wealthy lodge in mind shall not be identified by name for the same reason that jackpot Power Ball winners prefer to be anonymous. Thus, all that will be divulged is to indicate that it is in a big city on the East Coast and within easy driving distance of Washington, D.C.

This tale begins with an invitation to this author to give a talk at their big spring meeting. (The year is 1999; an important economic date to keep in mind.) At that time I knew nothing about this lodge. Their offer included flying my wife and me to the East Coast, putting us up overnight, paying a fat stipend for the lecture, then flying us home again after a couple of days of sight-seeing around the Capital. The whole deal sounded mighty good.

The time came. We arrived, were met at the airport and taken to our lodgings, then picked up and driven to their meeting place. Their rented meeting hall was located over a garage. Oh well, money must be tight; poor things. But how many Sons of Norway lodges in the U.S. gather together above a gas station and a garage?

The rather small upstairs meeting room was filled that night with members, so many that some had to sit on folding chairs out in the hallway, and some sat in adjoining siderooms where they could neither see nor hear well what was going on at their own lodge meeting. Oh well, poor things.

Time for the meal. It was a pot-luck supper. Obviously they could not afford a catered dinner, even if this was designated their special spring meeting of the year. Poor things. The pot-luck was good, of course (they almost always are). The presiding president whistled thorough the business proceedings, spending most of his time pleading for the members to get new and younger people to join. He then introduced the speaker for the evening (me), whose topic that night was the "Shifting Pattern of Published Writings About Norwegian Americans." Uff da. While the presentation produced some comatose bodies, the great majority there seemed genuinely interested in the topic as well as kindly laughing at jokes both good and bad.

Instant conclusion of the speaker upon at last sitting down: a good lodge! Too bad they're so short of funds. Oh well, poor things; hope they can limp along. Then a second conclusion: guilt. Guilt at taking their money and likely cleaning out their treasury. (Being both Norwegian and Lutheran made the guilt come easily.)

The gathering ended. When almost everyone had left the hall, the lodge treasurer called me aside to say he wanted to settle up with me. Yet one more conclusion: He probably wanted to renegotiate their initial offer. Oh well, poor things; better do it.

The treasurer began by telling about the struggling beginnings of their lodge, then about ten years old. "Yeah," he said, "we sure had a lot of bake sales and donated raffle items in those first years. It was tough to keep going," he added resignedly, and I thought, "Uh-oh, here it comes." He continued: "We finally got our treasury up to almost four thousand dollars. Then we got a new board member whose day job was that of a financial planner, and he asked and reluctantly got permission from the rest of the board to invest the lodge money into stocks."

("Uh-oh, risky Norwegians gambling on the risky stock market!")

He continued: "This investment guy said he knew a lot about computer companies and informed us later that he put almost all our money into Dell Computer common stock."

("Uh-oh, bet they lost every penny," I thought.)

He went on: "Well, then, before long this stock just . . . what do they say?—took off! And not only did its value keep shooting up, but the shares started to split and then split again."

("?")

"Purdy soon its value was up to $300,000.00."

("!")

"To our amazement, it just kept going up and up. It hit half a million bucks. It was getting embarrassing."

(I was getting embarrassed too about my earlier conclusions and false assumptions about poverty and penury.)

"When it hit $750,000.00 we didn't know what to do. We tried to keep it kinda quiet, but that's impossible. And now," he muttered more to himself than to me, "I s'pose we're worth about a million or so."

He then handed me a check for my costs and services. It was accepted with aplomb. Then this Country Mouse went back to the farm.

A Scandinavian immigrant in New York City, unable to find a job, set up his own lefse-making-stand on the street corner and sold each piece of lefse for a dime. Each day a well-dressed man walked by, left a dime, took no lefse, and walked on.

A week later the well-dressed man was stopped by the owner and was told: "I suppose you want to know why I left my dime and did not take a piece of lefse."

"Oh no," replied the Scandinavian, " I just wanted to let you know that I raised the price to 15 cents."

Soon the Centennial

FULL INDEPENDENCE FOR NORWAY FINALLY COMES IN 1905

Norway declared full national independence on June 7, 1905, thus proclaiming themselves dissolvent of a 91-year union with Sweden. A bold decision on the part of the Norwegian government. Would Sweden accept it? Prepared to fight, if necessary, both Norwegian and Swedish troops stood ready at their borders. Unnerving times for the Scandinavian world.

Independence for Norway had come in stages. Back in 1814 (on May 17, *Syttende Mai*), Norway had declared independence from Denmark after some 400 years of Danish control and proclaimed their own constitution. However, only months later, Norway found itself in a forced union with Sweden as a result of big power settlements made at the end of the Napoleonic Wars. While the accepted constitution allowed Norway almost full domestic controls, foreign policy was to be decided by Sweden.

Most Norwegians naturally disliked the fact that they had no say in their foreign affairs and were being represented abroad by Swedish diplomats. The issue of foreign policy as well as other key problems brought on dissatisfactions over the union, and these all came to a head with the proclamation of full Norwegian independence that spring of 1905.

Norwegian-Americans also reacted to the pronouncement in 1905 and responded with open support for Norway via letters, telegrams and petitions. For example, following a midsummer rally of thousands in the Twin Cities, two resolutions were passed, one to the Norwegian people for their "manly and calm" historic action, and one addressed to the Swedish people in America assuring them that good relations would continue.

However, the United States officially delayed any recognition of Norway's new status until Sweden announced its official response. This dallying upset many Norwegian-Americans who sent petitions to the then American president Theodore Roosevelt. The president, however, did not budge; he followed the safe position of watchful-waiting. Finally, that fall (October 27, 1905) Sweden acquiesced and formally recognized Norway's complete independence after nearly five months of suspense when the two countries were on the brink of war. Two days later, the United States followed suit with its own recognition of Norway.

Thus a fully independent Norway emerged as a new nation on equal footing with the rest of the free world countries. It was a long time a-coming. Nowadays, Norwegian-Americans also celebrate this monumental event by joining in with their own centennial celebrations in the year 2005.

"Sir, this train is not going to Minneapolis."

"No? Well don't tell me, tell the engineer!"

Outbesting the Best of 'Em

OH, BUT THAT WOMAN COULD TALK

For all of us, an unfortunate part of being alive is behavior that we have to acknowledge as sick or dysfunctional at worst, or just plain dumb at best. But exactly where the line separating emotional instability from egocentric behavior lies is not easily defined.

Or, as most of the men who sat on the bench in front of the barbershop said of Gladyce Osterholm, "She's nuts!" Only Arvid Buxengaard disagreed. "Nah, *nei-da*, Gladyce may act goofy, but her problem is that she's just so stuck on herself and only herself that she can't see or want to see anything else about anybody else but herself."

No doubt about Gladyce Osterholm's favorite subject: herself. Both the subject and her crassness on that subject were revealed in her famous line to the Watkin's man, a line tough to top: "Stop interrupting me when I'm interrupting you!" She had the kind of personality that could empty a room in fifteen minutes; ten, if she got on her medical problems. "Poor 't'ing," said her sarcastic neighbor, "she's got diarrhea of da mout'."

Gladyce was sixtyish, a big, raw-boned farm-wife, with frizzy, mousy hair that appeared to be combed with an eggbeater. Living two miles from town on a dairy farm, she also raised chickens—big Rhode Island Reds and little Bantams. The barbershop men saw a metaphor in those chickens, knowing which form of poultry her husband represented.

All the men felt sorry for the husband, Waldo, who yet was blessed with one ailment: he was hard of hearing. The bad news was that this made Gladyce talk extra loud, as though her audience was in the next county over. She always talked in CAPITAL LETTERS. Oh, but that woman could talk, not only at high volume but at high speed! "She can do 50 miles an hour with gusts up to 85," claimed Arvid, who had been thinking up a scheme to best her.

She would be tough to take on verbally because no matter what anyone said to Gladyce, regardless of the topic, she would immediately turn it back to herself. She never listened. At best she'd hear one word spoken to her and use that word as a springboard to launch into another screed. You could tell her that her neighbor's farmhouse was burning down this very instant and she'd respond by saying that reminded her of a fire that her pa once had in their corncrib. Local folks preferred talking to a stone wall rather than to Gladyce Osterholm because the wall wouldn't talk back and go on and on and on, yakkety-yakkety-yakking about nothing except her boring self.

Setting Up the Bet

Things were also pretty boring on the barbershop bench that morning until, sure enough, down the sidewalk came Gladyce on her way to the grocery store two doors away. Arvid then remembered his idea, really a proposal that he quickly turned into a bet with Omar Thuilen, the loser to buy two pitchers of Blatz beer for everybody at the tavern, one door away. A doozy of a plan.

Arvid's bet was that when Gladyce came back out again, he'd engage her in conversation, one in which he would say "special things," and the lines he used as illustrations were so appalling as to make some of the men shudder. "Ahhh, Arvid, yew von't say dose t'ings to her, den, vould you? Yeepers! She'll haul off and col'-cock yew!"

"Jus' you wait and see," replied a confident Arvid. "No matter what I say, my words will all go *whoosh,* right over her head," declared

Arvid, who at the same time made a high hand gesture to demonstrate the lost-words prediction. *"Whoosh,"* he repeated. "Stick around for our non-conversation."

The bet was set; the stage was set; the audience was in place, suddenly all sitting up and alert. The principal players were ready, too, as the star, Gladyce Osterholm, emerged from the store, arriving from stage right. Arvid knew his lines; Gladyce was expected to ad lib. It would be a memorable show.

The Clash of the Titans

"Helooooo, Mrs. Osterholm," cooed Arvid so fulsomely that Omar was ready to hand him an Academy Award. "You're looking good today," he purred.

'WELL I'M NOT FEELING GOOD. IT'S MY ARTER-ITIS ACTING UP AGAIN.'

"Y'know, I'm bothered by arthritis too and—" *Whoosh.*

'NOT LIKE ME YOU AIN'T. MINE'S SO BAD I CAN HARDLY CRAWL INTO THE SEAT OF MY PICKUP. OHHHH, THE PAIN . . .'

By the way, I poured some sand and gravel into your pick-up gas tank."

'YAH, I'VE GOT BAD GAS PAINS. YOU'D THINK THESE DOCTORS COULD PRESCRIBE SOMETHING FOR MY TROUBLES, BUT NOOOOOOO."

"I understand that your husband put some rat-poison pills in your coffee this morning." *Whoosh.*

'PILLS? I TELL YOU THESE YOUNG DOCTORS PUSH PILLS JUST TO MAKE MONEY, AND ALL THOSE PILLS DO IS GIVE ME HEARTBURN. OHHHH, THE MISERY . . .'

"Maybe we'll all get lucky and you'll have a heart attack and die." *Whoosh.*

'I'VE REALLY GOT BAD HEARTBURN. IT'S DRINKING TOO MUCH COFFEE WITH CREAM, AND COFFEE IS SOOOOO EXPENSIVE AND EGG PRICES ARE SOOO LOW . . .'

"Is it true that Waldo is one of those fruits who was caught making goo-goo eyes at your hired man in the cow barn?" *Whoosh.*

'I TELL YOU THAT IF COW PRICES DON'T GO UP I'M GONNA HAVE TO SELL MY PLACE AND END UP ON THE POOR FARM. YUP, THE COUNTY POOR FARM WHERE I'LL BET I GET BETTER MEDICAL HELP THERE, THEN; THAN HERE, THEN."

"Say, the men on the bench have been talking about mugging your sister, Mabel, Saturday night. Would you mind if we assaulted your sister?" *Whoosh.*

'OH, DID I TELL YOU THAT MY SISTER AND I TALK A LOT ABOUT GOING INTO A RETIREMENT HOME TOGETHER, WHICH IS LIKELY TOO, AS MY WALDO AIN'T LONG FOR THIS WORLD, THEN; AND THAT LOUT HUSBAND MY SISTER IS HITCHED TO SHOULD KICK THE BUCKET SOON, I HOPE. THAT CIGARETTE SUCKING, BEER GUZZLING NINCOMPOOP. A WORTHLESS SKUNK. YEW BETCHA, WHEN HE CROAKS IT'LL BE A BLESSING FOR US 'CAUSE ME AND MABEL COULD MOVE TO SUNSET HOME WHERE WE COULD PLAY BINGO EVERY DAY . . . "

The "theater audience" on the bench had found it hard to contain themselves throughout this production. Omar, in trying to suppress an outburst, started to cough loudly and began choking and getting red in the face. This vocal distraction was loud enough for even Gladyce to recognize and respond to accordingly:

'YOU SOUND LIKE YOU GOT THE CROUP, BUT LET ME TELL YOU ABOUT MY T'ROAT PROBLEMS . . ."

And then came the arranged sign of surrender from the coughing, gasping, laughing Omar who had reached into the bib of his striped overalls and came out with a five-dollar bill and waved it in the air. As though on signal, all the men arose and headed for the tavern, a smiling Arvid at the front of the thirsty line. Not so much as a single goodbye to the star of the show.

'BUT WAIT! LET ME TELL YOU ABOUT MY GALL STONES!—"

    Whoosh.

Background and Origins of the Norwegian flag

The official Norwegian flag has only existed in its present form since 1821, a relatively short time, and it has an interesting history.

The oldest-known Norwegian "flag" is a banner picturing a lion standing on its hind legs and carrying an ax in its forepaws. This royal banner was first recorded in 1318 and is still used by Norwegian monarchs today. The lion motif (red background, gold ax and lion) is repeated on the Norwegian National Coat-of-Arms.

In 1380 Norway entered into a union with Denmark because the same person became the heir to the thrones of both countries. Denmark was the stronger of the two and soon emerged as the dominating partner in the union. Hence gradually it became customary for Norway, too, to use the Danish flag, which is red with a white cross in the center.

It is understandable why the Danish flag was not appreciated by many Norwegians, who wanted to end the union and, among other things, achieve their own flag. That long union was finally dissolved in 1814 and Norway got its present constitution that year. However, not until 1821 was a design for a new national flag accepted.

The eventually accepted flag design was first presented by one Frederik Meltzer. He based his proposed flag on the Danish red and white flag, but within the white cross he placed a blue cross which symbolized liberty. This new, proposed flag thus represented

Norway's long history, notably its centuries with Denmark. The design was officially accepted and soon met with general public approval.

The political situation at that time (1821), however, did not allow this new flag to fly everywhere without changes. Norway had been forced to enter a union with Sweden in 1814. Although Norway was supposed to be an equal partner in this union, the Swedish king—who was in charge of foreign affairs for both nations—insisted that at least the large Norwegian merchant fleet must fly a flag that indicated their connection with Sweden. This ruling resulted in the Norwegian flag having a so-called "mark of union" in the upper left-hand square of the flag. This "mark" displayed both the Norwegian and Swedish (yellow and blue) colors and was referred to as the "herring salad flag" by contemptuous Norwegians who were appalled at their flag being sullied in such an ugly way.

It would take 91 years before Norway removed itself from the union with Sweden. When that union at last came to an end in 1905, it was a proud moment when the Norwegian pure red, white and blue flag was run up on flagpoles all over the country.

You know you grew up in a small town when you remember that you . . .

☑ . . . played "Kick the Can" and "Annie, Annie Over."

☑ . . . could name every member of your graduating class.

☑ . . . went to teenage parties at a barn, gravel pit or back road.

☑ . . . could not buy cigarettes because every clerk knew how old you were.

☑ . . . smoked your first cig—and had your first coughing fit—in an alley behind main street.

☑ . . . believed that any town with two stoplights was a big town, practically a city.

☑ . . . regarded the towns next to yours as either snooty or hicksville, but were actually just like your town.

☑ . . . had a nine-hole golf course with sand greens.

☑ . . . thought it cool to date someone from another town as any date from far away was automatically more sophisticated than the locals.

☑ . . . understood that planned events in town were timed so that the farm folks could get home in time to do chores.

☑ . . . knew what 4-H stood for.

☑ . . . thought that kids in the big city dressed funny, but you picked up the style two years later.

☑ . . . were positive that the same old men wore their same old blue suits to church every Sunday morning for the past 100 years.

☑ . . . saw at least one friend a week driving a tractor down main street.

☑ . . . had decided to walk for exercise and then had a half-dozen cars pull up beside you, the driver inquiring if you needed a lift.

☑ . . . regarded it as normal to see a guy driving through town on a riding lawn mower.

☑ . . . accepted as proper that the mentally retarded and the borderline insane not to be sent away; instead those folks were part of the community and taken care of by the whole community.

☑ . . . peed in a cornfield.

☑ . . . considered the spring spearing of suckers to be one of life's most exciting pleasures

☑ . . . never much thought about the notion that almost every one in town had a nickname.

☑ . . . had teachers who got you mixed up with brothers and sisters and cousins.

☑ . . . had teachers who bought all their beer and liquor in the next town.

☑ . . . understood that if there was big trouble at home, you did not call the police, you called your neighbor.

☑ . . . drove by the church at any hour of the day or night and felt the emending power from the silent structure reminding you to Shape Up.

☑ . . . observed that all the bibs in farmers' overalls had a circle in the top bib pocket made there by cans of Copenhagen chewing tobacco, i.e. snuff or snoose; yes, real men chewed snuff and really real men never spit.

☑ . . . decided once to become a real man and gave snoose a try; took a big pinch and packed it in your gums between your lower lip and your teeth, then waited for the thrills to kick in; the effects began when the world began to spin and you turned green; then you lay down and hung on tight to the revolving earth; got deathly sick, puked, and between heaves, resolved never to try that toxic stuff again.

☑ . . . believed strongly at the time that your hometown was the dullest, most boring alleged community in the entire uni verse; with age, however, it got better and finally improved to the point where it became a wonderful place in which to grow up.

Return of the Hometown Boy

AND THE SHAKEUP IN "SUNDAY SCHOOL THEOLOGY"

It is super special when a young person from a congregation chooses to go into the ministry. This does not happen often. For small-town Lutheran congregations, whose churches may have had their centennial years ago, it is still likely that over that long period the number of young people from any church who chose to become pastors can be counted on the fingers of one hand.

Thus it was a special Sunday indeed when their "Son of the Congregation," who recently finished his seminary training, agreed to come back home to conduct services in the same church where he had been baptized and confirmed; a church where he still knew 90% of the congregation—and they knew him. Understandably, the church was filled that day, except for the two front rows.

Church goers found it far easier to remember the young pastor, not as the valedictorian of his class, but more as the high school kid who drove like a maniac, who pulled power-u's on Main Street (the skid marks stayed for years). They recalled the kid who got caught by the sheriff for shooting off insulators from power lines; the kid who stole watermelons from Turkey Trinrud's melon-patch and gave them to the county food-bank. The kid who jauntily wore a pork-pie hat with holes cut in it. The kid who smoked those long Pall Mall cigarettes and got kicked off the basketball team for his smoking, even if he was the team's best player.

It was also easier to remember where the kid came from, that is, to know his straight-arrow parents, Kjetil and Gudren Rickensrud. (Behind his back, Kjetil's nickname was "Swivelneck," it being often said that he was so nosy that when he met someone while driving in his car, his head could swivel all the way around so that he could continue to watch the car through his own back window.)

This Sunday, however, Swivelneck's son was a 24-year-old graduate of the Lutheran seminary in Berkeley, California. (As the men on the bench in front of the barbershop said the next day, "If he had only gone to a . . . well, a normal, sane school, like ours in Saint Paul, he wouldn't have come out so . . . well, goofy.")

It Starts Safely

The early phases of the service went smoothly, so much so that the curious (read: nosy) congregation began to view him as just another visiting reverend filling in on a day when the regular pastor was on vacation. The young man read well and sang well; he even chanted well. He showed uncommon maturity in not rushing things, showing deference to the listeners by pausing just enough to allow all to find the appointed hymn or the correct page in the liturgy before continuing on. For this, Emil Gunderson whispered to the missus that "He's pretty good after all, for a young whippersnapper not dry behind the ears yet, then." Emil soon changed his mind.

The climax of the Lutheran service arrived; the young man moved into the pulpit to give the sermon. Until then he had made no allusions to his returning to his childhood home, his once being a part of their community. This changed with his first sentence in which he acknowledged his background and gave thanks to all for first asking him back to his home church and also for "collectively raising me as a child and as a normal, mixed-up teenager." He allowed that by this time, however, he did have his head on straight, and then he went on to talk about there being an advantage to outsiders who saw things differently on what might be done in making a Sunday·service different.

Upon hearing that last line, Oskar Thulien, normally settling in to doze (he called it "meditating") whenever any pastor mounted the pulpit, now opened his eyes, suspecting something special to follow. It did.

Safety is Abandoned

"It seems to me to be a pointless habit that the same people always sit in the same spot in the same pew every single Sunday, especially those who come early just to grab the back rows." Oskar stiffened, sensing what was coming. He was right.

"Just to try something different, I'd like to invite you folks in the two back pews to move up to the two empty front pews."

Nobody moved. Nobody breathed.

"I mean now. Hey, it's not so bad. Let's just try it. C'mon!"

Not surprisingly the decision to move began with the cantankerous Nils Torgrimson who got up and moved out the side door and down the steps and marched outside, huffing and mumbling to himself with every desultory step. No pulpit-pounder was going to tell him where to sit!

Back inside, the sustained silence was unnerving. Then finally when Astrid Pederson began to stand, the domino-effect began and the back-row-regulars, looking more sheepish than defiant, sidled forward, heads down, slouching ahead like condemned penitants towards the guillotine, in this case the empty pews in the very front rows.

"See now, that wasn't so bad," said the guest preacher and he laughed. Nobody else laughed. Picking up the bulletin, he then read the Gospel lesson for the day from Saint Mathew, and afterwards added: "By the way, nobody knows for complete certainty if the names associated with the four Gospels were actually written by men whose names are always connected to them." He looked out at perplexed faces and smiled, then added both levity and information: "In Norway their names are Mathias, Markus, Lukas, and Johannes." The perplexity hardened.

Well aware of the bewilderment, he apparently felt the obvious need for some kind of commentary: "What is most important is that the Gospels were written at all, not who wrote them." Some heads nodded; most never moved.

"As long as we're on the subject of names, it should also be made clear that the name Jesus is a man's single name. Just one name. It means 'He saves.' Jesus, the Savior. Therefore you should not believe his full name is 'Jesus Christ,' as though it were a name like Ole Olson. It technically should be 'Jesus The Christ,' Christ meaning the Savior or the Messiah. Do you follow the distinction?"

(This distinction was sort of brought up the next morning in the barbershop conversation when Telford Blekken added nothing to uplift the distinction by admitting when it came to names that he often wondered what the H. stood for in "Jesus H. Christ." And he was serious! Hans Rasmussen said that kind of stuff was disgusting and sacrilegious, but Telford didn't know what Hans' last word meant and he wasn't about to ask. To everybody's relief, Telford changed the subject to fishing.)

Young Pastor Rickensrud went on to not only acknowledge the value of his Sunday school experiences in general, but also to name some of his special teachers—Miss Voie, Mrs. Gudmandsen, Mrs. Floistad—and then thanked every teacher on behalf of every child fortunate enough to attend a Sunday school. "The power of a teacher of the young is immeasurable; teachers affect eternity. As the great church leader Ignatius Loyola proclaimed, "Give me the child and I'll give you the man."

(Helge Hanson said later that the idea about teachers might be true, "but did he have to quote that Catholic Jesuit?")

Safety is Tossed Out the Door

The guest pastor continued: "However, there would be a downside to my Sunday school experience and there is a need to raise that issue now." (What raised in the congregation were eyebrows.) "All in all I came away with a concept of God that was once imbedded in my mind so deep as to be hard to shake out when I became an adult, that is the idea/notion/belief that God was and is an old old man with a long white beard sitting on a throne with one hand holding a staff and the other hand gripping the arm of the chair."

He paused and looked out at a sea of very intent faces and then declared: "That is Sunday school theology that needs to be revised. Do you want a definition of God?" (Whether they wanted it or not, they knew they were going to get it anyway.) "Famous and brilliant German theologian Reinhold Niebuhr defined God this way: 'The ground of all being'." With that line a few folks grabbed the pencils used for filling out communion cards and scribbled furiously as the revision-lesson was extended: "God is the sacred at the center of existence, around and within us all. The nonmaterial ground of all being."

Another long pause. "Does that help?" No one nodded; no one moved. Then came the amendment: "Stop thinking of God as someone or something always 'out there'," and he pointed toward the ceiling and sky. "Instead start thinking of God as 'in here'," and he pointed at himself and also made a circling motion with his arm that was apparently meant to include the whole room, and any room anywhere. (Eyes wide open opened even wider.) "I had also considered discussing with you the cosmos but thought that that topic might be a bit confusing." (Some stunned heads nodded. No disagreement there.)

"And now I must take issue with another Sunday school lesson learned that should be unlearned. This topic is generally referred to as 'the inerrancy of the Bible.' My point here is that while Biblical accounts are written in archaic and redundant form, they are of historical value in describing the conditions at that time. However, it is evident that translators can and do make mistakes or have to pick words that do not convey the exact same meaning of the original. Then, when it gets translated yet again to another language, it may stray even farther from the original.

"Consider that the Bible was translated from ancient Hebrew to Aramaic to Greek to Latin to English. Therefore statements from ancient historical documents such as the Bible must not be taken at face value but checked against other sources of information. This should serve as an example to those religious groups or individuals who maintain every word in the Bible is 'inerrant,' infallible, free from error. To err is human and historical writings—like the Bible—have errors." (At that last line Mrs. Colrud was about to faint. At that point he might have entitled his sermon: "Good Thing I'm Here Today 'Cause I'll Never Be Asked Back Again.")

"By the way, the worst supposed quote so often attributed to the Bible is a line you've all heard hundreds of time: 'God helps those who help themselves.' If any of you can find that line, I will personally hand you a one-thousand dollar bill."

At Last the Sense to Quit

The young man at last and at least had the good sense to realize that his words—his revisionism, his shocks—had already been about as much of a sermon that the listeners could stand, let alone understand. He quit after talking only ten minutes. Normally such a short sermon was unheard of, but then never was there such a sermon heard in that church.

He left with a parting line that was more pointed than amusing: "Like the Christ, I came not to comfort the afflicted but to afflict the comfortable. To conclude: Sunday school is great; Sunday school theology is not great. Amen."

> An amazing, memorable Sunday in ways hardly anticipated. They expected pious platitudes but got upsetting theology.

This day there were no audibly repeated congregational "Amens," as is sometimes the case when a "sermon ends. Even if an amen—"may it be so"—was thought, it was not sounded. What sound there was was a collective sigh of Lutheran relief. It was over.

Most parishioners appreciated sermons that generated food for thought, but this new pastor had supplied them with enough meat and potatoes to last them a lifetime, maybe two lifetimes. An amazing, memorable Sunday in ways hardly anticipated. They expected pious platitudes, but got upsetting theology. All this in a culture of a town where virtually all citizens were nominally Christians and 90% were Lutherans. Any atheist remained silent in his disgusting position, and the town agnostic spoke only to his single counterpart in the next county.

So much to think about—and talk about. But God and Christ and the Holy Spirit were subjects never talked about any day of the week except Sunday, and on that day only the pastor did the talking. Between Sundays any lay person who mentioned the name of God, aside from the common daily swearing, in a thoughtful curious and/or moral or reverential or manner, was regarded by his fellow "Christians" as some kind of nut, a religious fanatic just one step away from being a holy-roller. A common put-down for those very few figures was to declare that they suddenly "got religion," implying that too much religion was bad for one, and that statement went on with "there's nothing wrong with that, of course," but of course there was.

Anyway, just don't talk seriously about religion; leave it all to the preachers. But that new sem-grad kid came along and made them think about God (sacred center of existence? out there? in here?) and possible errors in the Bible. Heavens! And how would he define heaven? He had invaded their minds, upset their solid Sunday school learning. All this confliction from one of their own who was supposed to come back just to conduct a ho-hum church service and let the locals see what he looked like. He looked good; it's what he said that was so usefully disturbing.

The first graders were being introduced to the topic of world religions, and four volunteers of different faiths agreed to bring to class the next day an "object of their faith" and hold it up for all to see. Next morning the four went up in front of their classmates.

The first one said, "My name is Abdul. I am Muslim and this is a prayer rug."

The second child said, "My name is Mary. I am Catholic and this is a rosary."

The third one said, "My name is Jacob. I am Jewish and this is a prayer shawl."

The fourth first grader went to the front of the room and said, "My name is Kari. I am Lutheran and this is a casserole hotdish."

Mysterious Surprises on a Foggy Night

The fog had tiptoed in to engulf the tiny main street, making the night so murky that it was difficult for the men to make out the Flying Red Horse sign looming high on the street corner in front of the small gas station. The closest street light was a dim yellow blur.

Inside three men sat around a balky oil-stove, sipping the last of their Dad's Root Beer, belching and farting and wondering out loud what time it was. After one reached to look, each in turn glanced at his own pocket watch, each watch attached to a leather string that was fastened to a brass button on their bib overalls, anticipating closing time coming soon to end another boring evening.

"According to my piece, it's 9:27," said Hans Ellingson.

"I got only 9:19, but I probably didn't wind it up tight enough this morning, then," admitted Knute Haukesvik.

"Well, then, seeing I gotta turn the key on this joint," said the owner, Martinus Anderson, "we'll go by my *klokke* and that says 9:25, and so, gents, we'll call it a day. My time-piece is right, of course. It comes from Norway, y'know. You wind it with a little key. My immigrant pa gave it to me just before he passed on then, y'know," and they knew because Martinus had told them that a hundred times or more. Might have thought it was a present from King Haakon himself.

"Sure gettin' foggy out there, then," observed Hans. "Well, another day, another dollar."

"*Nei* (No), more like a 50-cent day. Not much profit when gas sells for a quarter a gallon," lamented Martinus, who stood up to turn off the light switch on the half-hidden Flying Red Horse, and then he looked outside and could barely make out the bus creeping along and stopping by the sign. The bus came through every night, but it only stopped when it took on or let off passengers. Because neither one seldom happened, all three men got up and went to the window, staring intently to try to see through the fog enough to figure out who was coming to town.

Strangers in Their Midst

As they watched, the driver stepped out, then turned around to help down the steps a tall woman who was carrying a baby. The woman then turned around to help a little girl down the last step. When on the street, the girl grabbed the woman's long coat and hung on tightly. Next a small boy stepped off and he too huddled against the woman. The driver walked down along the side of the bus, opened a compartment and pulled out a large suitcase, carried it back and set it down beside the group. He tipped his cap, got back on, and the bus eased very slowly down the street and into the gloomy night.

The men looked at each other, each look suggesting the same question: Who's that? Shaking heads. No one knew. As lifelong residents they believed they knew everyone in their end of the county, but the lady with the three kids was a mystery.

Then the mystery started walking towards the station. Knute opened the door and once inside the four looked like one single statue, given the closeness of the kids hanging on. The woman's face revealed a strained and pained weariness; she looked so tired that she could have fallen asleep right there, standing up.

"Mr. Anderson," she said softly, "you likely do not recognize me now. You might remember me as Solveig Aakerson. My folks are on the old Thorson farm east of town."

Martinus looked again. "Sure'nuff. I know your ma and pa, and sure I remember you now, but, well, you kinda changed," he mumbled, looking as much at the dark kids as at her. The blond, blue-eyed mother stood out in contrast to the blackhaired, brown-eyed, brown-skinned children.

"My name is—or was—Solveig Garcia and these are my children: Fernando, he's six; Maria, she's four, and the little one is Juan Carlos; he's 14 months." The men concentrated on the words "is or was." Did

that mean now or before or later or what? Who's the father? The husband? Is there one now? If so, where is he?

"I s'pose you came to visit your folks, then," before blurting out, "Is your husband joining you soon?" Martinus did not know how to phrase it without showing how nosy he really was, and the other two men were glad he asked it as it saved them from asking it later.

"No," she replied, looking as though she was wondering herself how to respond. "Let's just say he's back in New Mexico."

The mystery seemed to be revealing itself just a bit. At this point the mother reached into the pocket of her long, threadbare coat and came out with a nickel. "I'd like to buy a bottle of soda. No, of pop, as you call it here, of Pepsi. We're all thirsty. We've been on and off buses for four days and nights straight. A long trip."

Martinus went to the metal cooler, lifted the lid, dug down amid the ice chunks in the cold water, and came up with a dripping bottle, wondering about 12 ounces for four people. He considered giving her two bottles until he heard her say: "It's so wonderful to be home to stay. And now a new place for my children to grow up."

The implications of that last line sunk in quickly. They're gonna settle down here? Those little Mexican kids gonna live here? (Their town had at best an uneasy toleration for outsiders in general, and strangers of another race was more than they could handle. Intimacy and neighborliness traveled side by side with intolerance and narrow mindedness.) No extra bottle was forthcoming.

The lone Pepsi was passed from hand to hand with the demurral of "Don't drink too much or too fast. Save some for the others." Begging brown eyes pleaded uselessly for more. The littlest one got the last drops although most of it ran down his double chin. "There, now we're refreshed," she declared. "Time for the last leg of our journey," and with that she rejuggled the position of the infant into her left arm, picked up the big, worn suitcase with her right hand, walked out the door, the kids shuffling beside her, and within seconds they disappeared, swallowed up in the dense fog.

Debating Social Policy

"Well what do you think of them berries?" said Martinus, more as a statement of shock than a question. The three stood staring out the window, and finally Knute muttered, "Sure a long walk. The Thorson place is at least two miles or more, and it's dark out there. Maybe someone should give 'em a lift."

But the other two had future shock in mind and not the present, not their plight, with Martinus declaring: "They don't belong here!" Hans added, "Yeah, why don't they go back where they come from? Just think, a bunch of Mexicans in town." Rolling his eyes, Martinus added: "Them Spics, they're about as bad as . . ." when Knute interrupted him: "They're not black, they're brown." That made a difference. In the black-white division of the American makeup, the added burden for Hispanics had historically been the perception of them as almost black or, at the very least, occupying an indeterminate place in the nation's racial mix. Whatever, among these agitated Scandinavians, they could have been Green Martians who were moving in on them.

"Well, if you ask me, Mexicans belong in Mexico. Period," declared Hans firmly.

"Now wait a minute," said Knute, "they're not Mexicans, they're Americans! Seems to me back in grade school we all memorized our

111

48 states and New Mexico was in there somewhere."

"Yeah, but they ain't white," Martinus responded, as though that line explained everything.

"They don't fit in here," added Hans, now standing up and pounding his fist into his other hand. "That's the problem. And think ahead about 20 years from now when they grow up here and plan to get married. Then what?"

"Then what?" Knute snapped back, now sitting on the edge of his chair. "I'm thinking back 20 years when my niece came here from Finland. She had dark skin and the kids in school made fun of her and called her a dumb Finlander and *Svart hode* (black head). They yelled at her and told her to go back where she came from."

"Yeah? So what happened?"

"She made it just fine, went to college and eventually became a lawyer. Then she married a doctor and they had two kids and they now live in the biggest house in town. Not bad for a dumb Finn, huh? Oh, and by the way, her husband's Jewish. Whadya think about that?"

"I think that shows our country is going to hell in a handbasket," said an agitated Hans.

"Oh?" answered Knute, now ready to lay on Hans something that he would never mention before. "Well, maybe you'd like to know that that's what your kinfolk said behind your Norwegian back after you married Ingrid Holten. It's bad enough for many that she's half Swede, but her other half is Heinz-57. Is it true that she's part Indian?"

"That's none of your damn business!" thundered Hans. "And who I married and what she is is none of your damn business, either. It's sumthin' between me and her, and that's the way it should be," he added firmly.

"Glad you said that and not me," Knute replied, satisfied. He then stood up and began to put on his denim barn-coat, then walked to the door. He turned back to announce: "If I've never done anything right in my life before this, I'm gonna do it now."

"Yeah? Like what?"

"I'm getting into my pickup and going after 'em, if I can find 'em, and give 'em a ride. Then we're gonna stop first at the cross-roads country store and I'm gonna buy those kids as much pop and candy and ice cream as they want. Then tomorrow me and the missus are going to the Thorson place with enough groceries to tide 'em over for a couple of weeks. How do you like them apples?"

"HAH!" snorted a disgusted Martinus. "Remember what they are, they're—" But he was not permitted to finish as he was interrupted by Knute, who said very deliberately: "They're a poor family who needs help right now," and then added, "This week I'm gonna go to the Pastor and tell him about them and I hope he will fill us half-assed Christians in church with enough Lutheran guilt to make us act like Christians instead of just mouthing pious piffle about 'helping those in need' on Sunday mornings and forgetting all about it by Sunday afternoons when the football games start."

> "I ain't much for memorizing Bible verses since confirmation classes but we all ought to look up Micah, chapter 6, verse number 8, and tattoo it to our foreheads."

Hans was pretending not to hear him, a good trick considering the volume of their arguments. Martinus relit his pipe for the tenth time and shook his head as Knute continued.

"I ain't much for memorizing Bible verses since confirmation classes but we all ought to look up Micah, chapter 6, verse number 8, and tattoo it to our foreheads."

Martinus kept shaking his head in woeful anticipation and mumbling something about "Damn do-gooders." But then he came back to reality, back to the here-and-now, back to the weather outside—remembering the blackness of the night and the near impenetrable fog. Martinus took sudden delight, believing that Knute would never find them. And when that first part of Knute's plan would fail, he reasoned, then he'd come to his senses and the rest of that liberal nonsense would collapse, too. "HAH!" he bellered again, "Bet you can't find'em in this fog. Best you forget about 'em. Let 'em go. Forget about the whole thing. Just look outside!" He did, and was aghast!

The three men walked to the front window. They looked out to see this time the Flying Red Horse sign shining clearly and brilliantly from the bright rays of the street light, now swaying back and forth in the strong wind.

The fog had lifted.

God asks only this—
To do justice,
To love kindness,
And to walk humbly
with your God.
—Micah 6:8

Jeg er Så Glad Hver Julekveld

I Am So Glad Each Christmas Eve

1. I am so glad each Christmas Eve,
   the night of Jesus' birth.
   Then like the sun the star shone forth,
   and angels sang on earth.

2. The little child in Bethlehem,
   he was a king indeed.
   For he came down from heaven above
   to help a world in need.

3. He dwells again in heaven's realm,
   the Son of God today,
   and still he loves his little ones
   and hears them when they pray.

4. I am so glad on Christmas Eve,
   his praises then I sing.
   He opens then for every child
   the palace of the King.

5. When mother trims the Christmas tree
   which fills the room with light,
   she tells me of the wondrous star
   that made the dark world bright.

6. And so I love each Christmas Eve
   and I love Jesus too,
   and that He loves me every day,
   I know so well is true.

Jeg Er Så Glad Hver Julekveld

1. Jeg er så glad hver julekveld,
   for da ble Jesus født.
   Da lyste stjernen som en sol
   og engler sang så søtt.

2. Det lille barn i Betlehem,
   han var en konge stor
   som kom fra himlens høye slott
   ned til vår arme jord.

3. Nå bor han hoyt i himmerik,
   han er Guds egen sønn,
   men husker alltid på de små
   og hører deres bønn.

4. Jeg er så glad hver julekveld
   da synger vi hans pris.
   Da åpner han for alle små
   sitt søte paradis.

5. Da tenner moder alle lys,
   og ingen krok er mørk.
   Hun sier stjernen lyste så
   i hele verdens ørk.

6. Jeg holder av hver julekveld
   og av den Herre Krist,
   og at han elsker meg igjen,
   det vet jeg ganske visst.

Provincial? Perverse? Perverted?

WHATEVER, SURPRISE GIFTS

The bestowing of gifts on any one at any time should be a pleasant experience for the person or persons receiving the present. Should be, but not always is. Sometimes surprise 'gifts' received and publicly revealed immediately to a surrounding audience brings reactions ranging from shocked amazement to shocked amusement to uncontrollable laughter to uncontrollable embarrassment.

For a roomful of watchers seeing these gag-gifts (one will be described shortly) for the first time, the responses will often be all of the above. No one could be neutral; no chance for faked apathy when the wrapping paper comes off.

One such illustration of a special 'surprise floral gift' was used in our hometown and never did the gift fail to elicit all of the above reactions to onlookers watching and/or participating in the the gift package being opened.

The wrapped package would always be big and tall and heavy because inside was a tall 'plant' in a tall vase. To drive home the point of its specialness, the outside wrapping of the plant would have a taped-on extra sheet of paper warning the recipient to be extra careful removing the covering-paper because of the delicateness of the dozen, long-stemmed "flowers" inside. The trap was then set. Time to reveal the "flowers."

And what were those "dozen long-stemmed flowers"? They were really 12 mature cattails pulled from some nearby swamp, all the stems cut off at the same long length. The extra uniqueness of this bouquet came with each cattail being enveloped by a rolled-down condom going far down the stem. (For variety, some givers preferred condoms of different colors). And dangling from the side would be a carefully printed card announcing in big letters: "POLISH RUBBER PLANT."

Two experiences with the above gift will be noted. Our neighbor, a woman who loved bizarre jokes, decided to give the "Rubber Plant" to her good friend on the occasion of the friend's 80th birthday party; the party held in a large party-room in a restaurant. Some 25 people—all adult women—attended the gathering and were dutifully seated as they watched the many cards and presents being opened, with the plant being the last gift to be revealed. With the honored guest standing beside the gorgeously wrapped present, she proceeded to pull off the paper with reckless abandon, at  the same time wondering out loud what on earth it might be. The final wrapping fell to the floor and the startling gift was revealed before all the intent watchers. At first there was silence, total silence; indeed, several quiet seconds went by. Then one lady in the back began to giggle and then another started to laugh and then another began to hoot; soon the entire room was roaring with laughter, with the birthday-child leading the guffaws. She later acknowledged that it would be a birthday gift that she would long remember.

A second experience involved this author who finally must 'fess up. The occasion was the 25th wedding anniversary of good friends who held the celebration in their home. There were many relatives and guests there, including their six children. To lend authenticity to the grand opening we arranged for a man—whom the wedding couple did not know—to deliver the plant/package, driving up to the house in a "delivery van." He also wore a chauffeur's cap, and with an air of a major business transaction he carried the plant to the door, then knocked and hollered "Special Delivery!" The couple accepted the gift with a touch of questioning in their faces, but they carried it in and set it on the table with the many other presents soon to be opened. Again the "plant" was saved for the last; after all it came special delivery. When the final wrapping was at last removed, the wedding couple stared awestruck with what they saw. At that moment the honored-husband's Norwegian background came out instantly with the loud line "*Herre Gud!*" (Holy God!); the honored-bride came forth with an incantation of her own to the deity, but howled it in clear English that needed no translation. Around them the guests were in stitches, all except their semi-grown children who wanted to laugh as hard as the rest but didn't dare to, what with their folks standing mummified before them. Since that memorable day—and it was indeed one to be remembered—the husband is still wondering who was behind this moment of surprise, and he will at last find out only when he reads this book.

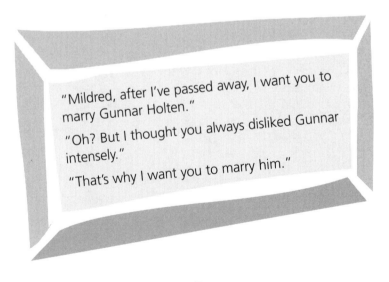

"Mildred, after I've passed away, I want you to marry Gunnar Holten."

"Oh? But I thought you always disliked Gunnar intensely."

"That's why I want you to marry him."

Art Lee in action

Talk, talk, talk

Caught twice in action, author Art Lee is shown addressing a crowd (and looking mighty formal). Also a picture of him teaching an Elderhostel class (appropriate map in background) on Scandinavian-America, with the catalog description reading: "Lutefisk and Lefse, Red Barns and Cream; Scandinavians and the American Dream." His second class was called "War, Wobblies, and Wild Wild Women".

The Blacksmith Who Never Talked

YET NEVER STOPPED TALKING

THE VILLAGE BLACKSMITH

Under the spreading chestnut tree
The village Smithy stands
The smith a mighty man is he
With large and sinewy hands
And the muscles of his brawny arms
Are strong as iron bands.
His hair was crisp and long and black . . .

No, not the hair. This is where the similarities in the poem ended for our blacksmith, whose shop we could see from the west windows of our elementary school. Our blacksmith had no hair on top, just a rim of white hair around on the sides. But he was strong, with an equally strong voice.

His blacksmith shop was a weathered clapboard building that had never experienced a single coat of paint, nor the windows a washing. At times the haggard structure looked more black than ugly gray. An eyesore either way. There were two sets of double doors that allowed entry and exit for machinery and tractors and horses, whatever blacksmith skills were required inside.

In the center of the dirty, plank-floored shop stood a pot-bellied woodstove, around which were placed items to sit on: empty nail kegs, potato crates, a plank between two saw horses—everything to sit on except for a real chair. Yet it was a daily gathering spot for the retired men of the village for at least a portion of each day when they were not on the benches in front of the barbershop or the ledge in front of the hardware store, or playing whist in the back rooms of the taverns, or at the post office hoping for some mail, any mail.

The men came not to talk, but to listen because the blacksmith did all the talking. A non stop talker whose volume went from loud to louder before reverting back to loud again. A newcomer would have thought that everyone sitting there around the stove was hard of hearing, which may have been close to the truth. Even child listeners accompanying their dads or grandpas got hollered at (and scared), not because they were being bawled out; that's just the way the smith's words came out.

Wearing a leather apron over his bib-overalls, and with his sweat-soaked denim shirtsleeves rolled up above the elbows, the smith daily pounded the red-hot irons on his anvil with heavy hammers, and he turned the crank on the bellows in the forge, and during all that time and motion he talked. And talked. And sometimes he shouted and laughed too loud and told anecdotes and off-color stories. He was a jokester. Sometimes. Maybe. Folks could not always tell when he was joking or serious; then again was he ever serious?

The man had penetrating gray-blue eyes, but those eyes never betrayed his real feelings. He could be shoeing a horse or grinding a cultivator blade or wrenching a stubborn nut off a binder wheel, all the time talking, talking, sometimes looking directly at his audience. But always his hawk-like stare never changed.

This hearty, outgoing, laughing, hail-good-fellow man, so gregarious, gave daily secular sermons in which he bestowed, whether they wanted it or not, voluble opinions on everybody and everything. He could and would pontificate, making Mt. Zeus pronouncements on all subjects, be it weather, politics or the war.

The war: World War II. The war was going on and the blacksmith had two sons, both in the army, one a pilot in the air force. The year was 1944. The news burst through town: the younger son had been piloting a B-24 bomber in a squadron ferrying planes from America to Great Britain and his plane crashed into the ocean about 100 miles from its destination, killing all on board. He was 21 years old.

The blacksmith shop stayed open; it was not closed a single working day, including Saturdays. The shop stayed the same; the blacksmith stayed the same. How he felt, what he felt about the death of his son he never said to anyone. No one. He didn't want to talk about it; he didn't talk about it—ever!

Yet he did keep talking, talking, talking loudly in his shop about the same things he had talked about before the monumental personal tragedy in his family. The retirees kept coming in daily and found their nail kegs to sit on and listened and watched the sweat dripping from his bald head while he held forth. His manner

> **He continued to entertain his listeners with stories, sometimes talking in Norwegian, sometimes a mixture of English-Norsk.**

remained overwhelming. He continued to entertain his listeners with stories, sometimes talking in Norwegian, sometimes a mixture of English-Norsk. Whatever, the monologues continued; the mirth continued; the show went on. He laughed loudly at a time when his audience expected him to throw back his head and let out a terrible scream of overwhelming sadness. No screams; just mirth.

That year, 1944, I was an eighth-grader in the school just across the street from the blacksmith shop. We walked by the shop every day and every day we could hear the noise of the pounding and grinding going on inside; we could also hear his stentorian voice. A boisterous man. On occasion we'd stick our head inside the door and he'd spy us and shout at us and try to be funny. We knew what he would do; we expected it, knowing his crusty intensity did not mean anger. He was just, well, himself, and not funny at all.

In eighth grade you don't know how people are supposed to react and respond when one learns that his son has been killed. Still, even then I thought it strange that the blacksmith seemed on the surface to be so unaffected, so unchanged, as though nothing had happened. I wondered then about the blacksmith; I still wonder now.

Another author originally from my hometown, Dr. Lowell Peterson, also wrote about the blacksmith in his recent book and gives this assessment: "I began to understand, as I grew older, the sadness in the old [blacksmith's] eyes I had seen as a child. I also understood more fully how he handled the loss of his son, by beating the metals into beautiful, useful forms while controlling his audience, and making his natural humor a positive force in his life and in the lives of us all." Peterson is a semi-retired heart specialist who lives in Appleton. He has acquired an intense interest in the lives of WW II P.O.W.s, mainly from Waupaca County, and he did extensive interviews with several of them. The result is a fine, moving (sometimes chilling) book he called *The Sun Rose Clear: Stories of WW II*, as told to and by Lowell Peterson (available at Peterson House, 2627 Beechwood Ct., Appleton, WI 54911). In that book Peterson has a chapter on the blacksmith and always refers to him by name—Irving Gottschalk (1884–1962); he also has photographs of the man, his shop and a picture of some men sitting around the stove. Peterson and I have remained friends over the years. In an earlier book, *Leftover Lutefisk*, I wrote about winning the "Big Game" when he and I were on the same Sunday-afternoon town baseball team. In the book he is referred to as "the handsome first baseman" who scored the winning run.

"Truls, haff yew effer noticed how miny towns are named efter der water towers, then?"

123

STATE OF MINNESOTA
DEPARTMENT OF CONSUMER AFFAIRS

JOB OPPORTUNITY: Lutefisk Inspector II

SALARY RANGE: $1,295 to $1,895 annually!

The State of Minnesota is seeking to establish a list of persons who qualify for the position of Lutefisk Inspector II. This is not an entry level position and requires experience and/or education. Please complete the questions below as required in the initial qualification screening for this position.

First Name: ___Sven ___Knut ___Ole ___Torvald

Last Name: (your pa's 1st name–if you know who your pa was)

_____son/sen (cross out as appropriate)

Address:
General Delivery_____MN Zip_____ (If not yet memorized, put 0)

Residence Type:

___Boat	___Barn
___Pier	___Pick up Camper
___Culvert	___Ice Fishing House

Spell *lutefisk* in the space provided: _____

Highest grade completed: 1   2   3   4
Number of years required to complete: _____
(If older than the teacher, put an X)

Related work experience:

___Deckhand	___Tanner
___Fish Baiter	___Herring Choker
___Fish Monger	___Dead Fish Identifier
___Boat Puller	

Number of years experience:

___1 to 5   ___5 to 10   ___10 to 20

___Need more fingers   ___Need more toes   ___Need both

Equipment qualified to operate:

___Fork Lift   ___Fork   ___Flush Toilet

___Pencil   ___Retractable Pen   ___Kleenex

___Garbage Can   ___Doorbell   ___Doormat

___Snoose Can   ___Lottery Machine   ___Bait Caster

Foreign Language Proficiency:

___English   ___Minnesotan

___Norski   ___Ya Sure

___Heyya   ___Svenska

If you claim previous experience in consumption of lutefisk, show date and hospital at which you were treated:

_____

In your own words (at least three in same language) state why you want this position:

_____

_____

_____

Remembering the Music Man

A REAL ONE

He was a Music Man. That simple, almost banal designation gets tossed off easily as part description, part explanation, part compliment. It is, of course, applied to someone connected with music in general, but in particular one directing bands and choruses.

If the line is slightly altered to "He was a real Music Man," then there's a specialness indicated of that person's interest in and dedication to organizing and directing performing musicians. Our man was a real Music Man.

Obviously there were and are and will be hundreds, likely thousands of Music Men as long as there are public schools, colleges and universities, as well as willing post-school participants who still enjoy singing and/or playing an instrument.

Music Men come and go. Many have their moments, even their years of public recognition and appreciation, but then comes retirement, aging, and they're out of the public eye. Too soon they're forgotten. Men who start as young Music Men become middle-aged Music Men, then become old Music Men, then retired Music men, and finally forgotten Music Men by the time they pass on. Such is the pattern. Such is life.

However, there are those few directors who transcend this mundane pattern and are remembered at the end in the most remarkable, most wonderful, most touching way.

His name was Theodore Wilhelm Thorson, but he was regularly referred to and identified by the initials "T.W." A child of Swedish immigrants, he was born on a farm near Winthrop, Minnesota, in 1894. After high school, T.W. attended the University of Minnesota and graduated with a degree in agriculture in 1916. (He became a U "letterman," throwing the shotput on the track team.) The next year he went into the U.S. Navy where he served as a musician and bandmaster. At war's end, he moved to Fisher, Minnesota, a small town in the center of the Red River Valley, to teach high school

Ted Thorson. The band was with him to the end.

agriculture. There he met and eventually married the high school home economics teacher, Lillian Erikson, whose parents also were Swedish immigrants. They would have three children: Ted Jr., Marilyn and Keith.

T.W. had a life-long passion—indeed, a missionary complex—to promote music. In his first year of teaching, he not only started the band in his own school, but started bands in two neighboring towns, also. The couple moved first to Fertile before their final move to Crookston in 1929, and there he was in charge of the entire public school music program. This "take charge" director was a big man, standing six feet tall and on the robust side at 220 pounds. But he never looked portly because of his bearing and manner. He stood tall and straight—and insisted to any and all whom he directed that they do the same. Never ever would he permit slouching, whether standing or sitting.

He directed Crookston's school bands and choirs. He directed the community band and choir; he directed the summer band; he directed his church choir. His dedicatory missionary work in making new converts might be seen in his giving personal lessons on Saturdays for 20 years to over 1,600 students, at no charge to the students.

Then there were the musical groups outside of town that he organized. Scandinavian immigrants came to America with their tradition of male choruses. Naturally T.W. would organize and direct his local Odin Male Chorus, but he organized Scandinavian singing groups in the neighboring towns, too. Then once each year all the choruses would combine—175 men—becoming the Northwest Singers Association, directed by T.W. Thorson, and for 20 straight years they were featured in the Red River Valley Winter Shows.

T.W.'s sons, Ted Jr. and Keith, both recalled later that their first major thrill in music came with their singing in their dad's Northwest Chorus. "Not only did one hear thrilling choral music," said Keith, "you could feel it go right up your spine." (Although retired as an aeronautical engineer, music is still in him. At age 77, Keith was still playing weekly gigs with his clarinet. He said it was inherited: "It's all in the genes.")

There were other groups, too, but one very special organization was the Ninth District Legion Band, which T.W. first organized in 1928. He stayed with them, and they with him, literally to the end, 45 years later.

The legion band was different in many ways. The membership, from all over northwest Minnesota, was always changing, making it extra difficult for the director, and yet there was responsibility by most members, if not devotion. Retired from the military, many members drove long distances in all kinds of weather to make rehearsals, play concerts and march in parades. They participated because they wanted to, and almost all members were good musicians (many high school band directors in the legion band).

The legion band members also played hijinks. While playing and marching in some summer weekend parades, it was not uncommon for a few of the marchers to march away from the group and march into the nearest barroom. There, after a quick bump and a beer, they would hurriedly march out again and rejoin the band, by then far down the next block.

The quality of the legion band is noted by their fourteen times being selected as state champions at the annual state convention. In their spiffy-looking uniforms, they both marched well and played well and were regularly chosen at these conventions as the featured band for the Evening Memorial Service. They would end the program with a march appropriately named "The Vanished Army," but for the service the number was played with slow cadence and with muffled drums

Someone who had joined the Crookston faculty in the late 1950s said, "By then T.W. Thorson was already a legendary figure in the community and the region." She added: "It's easy for outsiders to dismiss someone by calling him a big frog in a small pond. Well, for T.W., this was one huge frog who dwarfed the puddle." She added: "He was a handsome man with real presence, and he loved, simply LOVED, band music." (Comments made by Lorraine Cecil, now retired from Bemidji State University. Her late husband, E. James, a WW II vet, played for years in the Ninth District Legion Band, and he had told his wife: "We played tough, quality music. It was an honor to play for that man.")

Aside from his many musical connections, T.W. was also a leader in community services, among which included membership—and presidency—of the Rotary Club. In World War II, when the National Guard was called into military service, T.W., as a Captain, organized the Crookston Area State Guard. During the Korean War, he organized the Third Battalion of the State Guard; by then he had been promoted to Lieutenant colonel. For his overall civic contributions, he was the recipient of the Golden Deeds Award, presented to him directly by the Governor of the state, C. Elmer Anderson.

T.W. Thorson's multiple activities wound down slowly as he advanced in years. Little by little he let go, first with his official retirement from the public school position, then after that he gradually withdrew from one organization, then another, then another . . . . It appeared that the pattern of Music Men moving towards semi-obscurity might move in on him, too. People forget fast. Out of sight, out of mind. His life had settled down and his days were dwindling down as he moved close to his 80th birthday.

Until that last autumn, his general health had been good. However, precipitated by hornet stings, he was hospitalized, and suddenly and dramatically his condition worsened, then became critical. He died of heart failure on September 23, 1973. A good man gone; a fine man whose passing would be mourned by his family and perhaps by a faithful few; a legend done with; another Music Man slipped away. Time to forget him. Hadn't most folks already forgotten?

A proper funeral followed, held in his beloved Trinity Lutheran Church. A touch of days-long-gone-by came with a hymn sung by about a dozen men, all in their 80s or older, who had once sung in T.W.'s Scandinavian Male Chorus. The pastor even added a touch of levity in his funeral message by suggesting at one point that likely T.W. was already in heaven "arguing with F. Melius Christianson as to who had the best arrangement of 'A Mighty Fortress Is Our God'."

The service ended. It was all very nice, very traditional, very proper— almost over. All that was left was the final obligatory drive to the cemetery, the extended family members and maybe a few special friends to serve as escorts to the burial.

Guided and led by the funeral director, the family members left their front row pews and slowly walked down the long church aisle behind the casket leading to the opened double doors at the front of the church and the entrance area standing high above the street below.

When the family came to the entrance and looked down, they saw it; they saw them, saw them all standing there at attention in their uniforms, standing there in perfect order, row after row, their instruments held ready—no slouching. The Ninth District Legion Band had quietly assembled in front of the church to give their former director one last grand march, one last grand parade, one last grand sound of a marching band to escort the Music Man to his final resting place.

In the last row of the band was a line of men who held no instruments. Instead they held canes and crutches and walkers; and yet they too were standing at attention, standing as erect as their frail bodies would permit. And one man was sitting at attention in his

The Ninth District Legion Band wins first prize in a competition in Virginia, Minnesota, in 1937. Leader Ted Thorson is fifth from the right.

wheelchair. They were former band members who still had one last march in them for their former director.

It was a grand sight! T.W.'s oldest son, T.W., Jr., would say later: "When the services ended and we came out the church doors and looked down on that street scene, it was the most moving, the most powerful experience I've ever had." His wife Margaret added: "It was absolutely breathtaking."

The funeral procession began to move slowly. On this warm, beautiful, September afternoon in Crookston, Minnesota, this large funeral procession eased forward from the church towards downtown. The legion band began to play, playing their appropriate signature song, "The Vanished Army," and the tempo for this occasion was deliberate, somber and stately, as were the marchers; as were the watchers standing on the sidewalks on both sides of a crowded main street. The grand procession marched right through the center of town before winding their way to the cemetery in a final moving tribute to a very unforgotten Music Man.

Such a funeral procession had never before been seen in that community, nor has there been anything close to it since.

Singing With the Lutherans

BY GARRISON KEILLOR

I have made fun of Lutherans for years—who wouldn't if you lived in Minnesota? But I have also sung with Lutherans and that is one of the main joys of life, along with hot baths and fresh sweet corn. We make fun of Lutherans for their blandness, their excessive calm, their fear of giving offense, their constant guilt that burns like a pilot light, their lack of speed and also for their secret fondness for macaroni and cheese. But nobody sings like them.

If you ask an audience in New York City, a relatively "Lutheran less" place, to sing along on the chorus "Michael Row the Boat Ashore" they will look daggers at you as if you had asked them to strip to their underwear. But if you do this among Lutherans they'll smile and row that boat ashore and up on the beach . . . and down the road!

Lutherans are bred from childhood to sing in four-part harmony. It's a talent that comes from sitting on the lap of someone singing alto or tenor or bass and hearing the harmonic intervals by putting your little head against that person's rib cage. It's natural for Lutherans to sing in harmony. We're too modest to be soloists, too worldly to sing in unison. When you're singing in the key of C and you slide into the A7th and D7th chords, all two hundred of you, it's an emotionally fulfilling moment.

I once sang the bass line of "Children of the Heavenly Father" in a room with about three thousand Lutherans in it. And when we finished we all had tears in our eyes, partly from the promise that God will not forsake us, partly from the proximity of all those lovely voices. By our joining in harmony, we somehow promise that we will not forsake each other.

I do believe this: people, these Lutherans, who love to sing in four-part harmony are the sort of people you could call up when you're in deep distress. If you're dying, they'll comfort you. If you're lonely, they'll talk to you. And if you're hungry, they'll give you tuna salad.

Want to be Scandinavian?

BE MODEST AND LEARN TO TALK RIGHT

"Scandinavians are a very modest people" is an assertion that is, I believe, basically true. That opinion is, of course, a generalization, but then generalizations are generally true.

"But they have much to be modest about" is also an assertion, but said with tongue-in-cheek, and thus becomes almost a throwaway line—and also not true. Final assertion: collectively Scandinavians and Scandinavian Americans have been and remain good people, good citizens. (There, I said it and I'm glad.)

Although impossible to pinpoint exactly why there is validity in the above assertions, those opinions most likely came from growing up and living in a Scandinavian climate and culture that teaches/preaches modesty as a major virtue. (It's likely the first explanatory footnote that appears just below The Ten Commandments.) Conversely, arrogance is not only an undesirable trait, it's a sin. (That's the second footnote.)

Within the definition of arrogance is "showing off." Don't. Bad form. Best to drive a Ford or a Chevy. There was a wonderful, wacky idiom used for those who did attempt some form of showing off, namely "They're tryin' to put on the dog." That's no compliment.

Modesty, self effacement, avoiding forwardness and loudness and any disposition to call attention to yourself were values insisted upon. It's all right to be good, but not too good as that presents problems.

Consider that even the King of Norway, Harold V, chose to go on television at the end of the Winter Olympic Games in Lillehammer and apologize to the world for their winning too many gold medals!

How to Talk Scandinavian

Scandinavians learn to talk about themselves indirectly. They grow up to be afraid of sounding arrogant when using the first person singular, and thus the single word "I" is often avoided, resulting in some loopy syntax. It leads to dropping the subject of a sentence and going straight to the verb. Examples: "Went to town last night. Had a hamburger. Drove home." "Hey, saw you in a new pickup. Liked the color." "No. Don't wanna eat no broccoli."

This phobia against the dreaded pronoun "I" gets reinforced when hearing ongoing criticisms aimed at those few sinners who somehow avoided the message: "Yeah, listen to that guy when he talks, then. He's got a big 'I' problem. Stuck on himself. A regular braggart."

Along with forced modesty are correlative behaviors, notably noncommittal answers as well as a penchant for privacy in words and thoughts. With these come the use of a phrase that gets learned at an early age; it is useful and safe in almost any situation in which a judgment is required. This panacea comes with mumbling two magic words: Not Bad. When stated, not bad does not necessarily mean that it is good; it's just that it's, well, not bad. Sample situation:

> **Consider that even the King of Norway, Harold V, chose to go on television at the end of the Winter Olympic Games in Lillehammer and apologize to the world for their winning too many gold medals!**

"So how was the movie last night?"

"Not bad."

The film could have been atrocious. Appalling. Monumentally putrid! Then again, the movie could have been wonderful! Superb! Fantabulous! The questioner may never know—and likely wasn't supposed to know—when the answer is the murky but useful not bad.

(What were the last dying words of the Scandinavian whose doctor asked him how he was feeling: "Not bad.")

Some readers may shake their heads in wonderment at trying to understand this verbal goofiness. Any explanation includes growing up in, and absorbing an atmosphere where one learns early that its safer not to say exactly what one thinks or believes or feels. Pure honesty is just for little kids. Don't share. Don't talk. (Scandinavians do not make good talk show hosts. This may also be applied to some husbands. Nels Peterson loved his wife so much that he almost told her so.)

Attempts to Explain

It is impossible to get even close to an agreed-upon definition of Not Bad, knowing that the term has far ranging uses from weather conditions (not bad) to fishing successes (not bad) to the amount of money one got when selling the pickup (not bad). There are, of course, various spinoffs, starting with Not Too Bad, which phrasing suggests a slightly more positive modification. "How was your trip to the city?" "Not too bad."

Sometimes Interesting is substituted and and that single word is even a more wonderful way to cop-out with any honest, forthright reply. Illustration: "How was the high school concert?" Answer: "Interesting." This could mean that the concert was so bizarrely awful that one wonders why any sane person with normal hearing would show up for five minutes to be atonally assaulted by this alleged musical cacophony. Then again it could have been an excellent concert. Whatever, it always safest to say that anything is interesting.

Pretty Fair, and Fair-To-Middlin connote some degree of success, without tipping one's hat too far, as it were. Sample: "So how'd you do picking blueberries along the swamp road?" Answer: "Oh, fair-to-middlin'." Another near substitute, with just a shade of betterment suggested, is Not Too Shabby, as perhaps applied to the quality of work done by the mechanics at the Ford garage.

Useful answers, useful euphemisms all, all too easily applied to the

Scandinavian character and characteristic of maintaining one's privacy. Remain stolid but solid. That's not bad.

But Aren't All Families Alike?

No effort will be attempted (wasted?) to justify, let alone promote, the notion that Scandinavians are necessarily any better than any other ethnic group. They're just, well, different. Sometimes they don't realize as much, however. Here's one illustration only of a young man's awakening to this realization; a true tale told to this author:

The young man grew up in both a Scandinavian household and neighborhood. His parents were both second generation Americans and the family socialized mainly with extended family members, i.e. grandparents, aunts/uncles, cousins, assorted in-laws, all gathering together usually on holidays.

Indirectly over the years the young man learned about Scandinavian names, foods, celebrations, expected behaviors, social graces, low-keyed humor, religious habits, proper hospitality, grieving responses, etc., although cultural heritage and maintenance were never overtly pushed or promoted. The sneaky lessons were all gleaned from observing and listening.

All this time the young man's home life was stable and secure; there was almost no parental acrimony, at least never in front of him. Seldom did anyone raise their voice; there seemed to be just one modest level of talking and acting in all they and the the extended family did. Even-tempered. Never pushy. All right to laugh, but not too loudly; all right to argue, but not too loudly. Everyone, everything always under control. Reticent. Phlegmatic. Keep the level level. And don't complain. Life may be unfair, but don't bellyache about it.

Although the young man rarely thought about it, he figured that he was probably loved, although neither parent ever told him as much. By the time he reached young adulthood, he concluded that the relationships with and within his larger family was also pretty good. Everyone got along well enough in that they were all courteous and respectful of one another, including semi-tolerance for all opinions; few argued at all, let alone forcefully. Moderation in all things, whether dressing or drinking or eating or (as his cousin Arnold whispered to him) having sex; but never talk about the latter. And EVERYBODY seemed conservative (read: tight).

Certainly none of this touchy-feely stuff went on between or among his extended family. P.D.A.s? (Public displays of affection); never. How about at home? Heavens, no! He had never seen his parents kiss, and almost no overt affection towards the son, either, although his mother would on occasion pat his hand in a gesture of love and kindness. His silent father kept his physical distance except for the times when they would shake hands formally during the young man's going to and coming home from college. His college graduation day produced a special two-hands handshake from the father.

Hence, on the basis of the Scandinavian life and lifetime he experienced, he had to conclude: So that's what parents are like; what families are like; what life was like for this new adult ready to leave home and start his new job; ready to go out on his own; ready to think seriously about getting married and starting a family of his own, which would be just like his own family. They're all like this, aren't they?

Then the shock came; then the awakening happened; then all former assumptions flew out the window because then he married into an Italian family.

Uff da.

The End is Near/Here

Finally we come to the end of this book, the moment when the reader closes the covers, the moment when a judgement is rendered, the moment when the author hopes that that judgement might at least reach the level of Not Bad. If so, hey, you've joined the group; now you're an honorary Scandinavian.

Art Lee

About the Author

Art Lee recently received another award, this one from his alma mater at Luther College, Decorah, Iowa where at the 2003 Fall Homecoming Ceremonies, he was presented with The Distinguished Service Award by the President of the College.

Among the major factors in his being chosen for this award were the many books he has written (this book is the tenth) dealing with Scandinavian American life and culture in general, and Norwegians in particular. (Luther College was founded by Norwegian Americans in 1861.)

A retired history professor from Bemidji State University, Lee believes that history is too mistakenly thought of as a dry subject that's always about Presidents or Politicians or Wars or Tariffs with Dates and more Dates to memorize. Not so, says Lee; "History is about people."

(Nor was history defined correctly by one of his students who, when asked to define history, blurted out that "History is just one darned thing after another.")

Too often readers—and writers—assume that the only history worth commenting on is the history of others always faraway, and of course always about "important" national and world figures.

Maybe, says Lee. But while the Big Histories concern themselves with the changing patterns in world and American civilizations, it is the Little Histories—the lives and events that go on unspectacularly in daily human relationships—that both affect and interest most people. Thus, Lee writes about plain small-town folks as they relate to each other and their community. Relationships: That's Real History.

No relationships anywhere, nor on any level, nor at any time period are perfect, of course. Life is full of ups and downs, good moments and difficulties, happy memories and sad memories. Reading about this makes us both think and think back as Lee's narration touches the nerve of remembrances in our own lives. As we read his commentaries, we're sometimes amused, bemused, confused, and sometimes saddened and moved—but never bored. He invites us to share in what some folks want to label "The Good Old Days," all the time knowing that "The Good Old Days" are now.

And now, lastly, for some modest
Scandinavian parting advice:

Put a little water on the comb.